I0644677

Successful Digital Painting

Unlock the secrets of digital painting with this comprehensive guide designed for artists at every level. Whether you're a beginner struggling to bring your visions to life or an experienced artist looking to refine your skills, this book offers invaluable insights and practical advice. From mastering the fundamentals to exploring advanced techniques, you'll find everything you need to create stunning digital artwork.

Dive into the world of digital painting with step-by-step tutorials, expert tips, and inspiring examples. Learn how to navigate the complexities of digital tools, understand the principles of light and shadow, and develop your unique artistic style. With clear explanations and detailed illustrations, this book demystifies the process and empowers you to achieve your creative goals.

Discover the importance of practice, the value of learning from mistakes, and the joy of continuous improvement. This book is not just a technical manual; it's a source of inspiration and encouragement, reminding you that every artist's journey is unique and filled with opportunities for growth. Embrace the challenges, celebrate your progress, and let your creativity flourish.

Whether you're working on character design, environment art, or any other digital painting project, this book is your trusted companion. With its practical guidance and motivational insights, *Successful Digital Painting* will help you transform your artistic dreams into reality.

Gilles Beloeil is a professional concept artist and illustrator who has been working in the gaming industry since 2007. Prior to his transition to concept art, he spent approximately six years in the visual effects industry as a lighting technical director and digital matte painter on various films and TV series. He is best known for creating some of the most iconic concept artworks for the *Assassin's Creed* franchise, a role he held for nearly 15 years. He has also been teaching an environment painting and design class online since 2015.

Successful Digital Painting

What You Need to Know

Gilles Beloeil

CRC Press
Taylor & Francis Group
Boca Raton London New York

CRC Press is an imprint of the
Taylor & Francis Group, an **informa** business

Designed cover image: Gilles Beloeil

First edition published 2026
by CRC Press
2385 NW Executive Center Drive, Suite 320, Boca Raton FL 33431

and by CRC Press
4 Park Square, Milton Park, Abingdon, Oxon, OX14 4RN

CRC Press is an imprint of Taylor & Francis Group, LLC

ISBN: 978-1-032-88219-2 (hbk)
ISBN: 978-1-032-88218-5 (pbk)
ISBN: 978-1-003-53670-3 (ebk)

DOI: 10.1201/9781003536703

Typeset in Minion
by Apex CoVantage, LLC

Contents

FIGURE 0.1 Digital painting done in Photoshop for *Assassin's Creed Unity* (*Assassin's Creed* TM & © Ubisoft Entertainment. All Rights Reserved).

Introduction

DOI: 10.1201/9781003536703-1

Painting can feel overwhelming, especially at the beginning. There's so much to learn and keep in mind that the process can become extremely stressful. You watch your favorite artists producing incredible work, while you spend days struggling with an image that—without knowing why—seems destined to remain lost in a file on your computer, never ready to be shared. You invest tremendous effort, only to feel disappointed or even disheartened by the results.

At this point, you face two options: either you give up on your dream, or you seek help from those who've been through this journey before you. The good news? That help is right here in your hands. This book is a modest but sincere contribution—one that aims to be among the many sources of guidance and support that encourage you not to give up.

Painting isn't witchcraft, even though its results can sometimes feel magical. There's a lot to learn, study, and practice—but it's doable.

You're likely searching for shortcuts, insights, or elusive techniques that your favorite artists seem to possess—knowledge that feels just beyond reach. That quest is a meaningful moment filled with anticipation, curiosity, and a desire to understand how these stunning works come to life.

Self-teaching is deeply rewarding, but it also takes time. This book is designed to guide you on that journey and save you time by offering the essential knowledge you need to move forward with confidence.

FIGURE 0.2 Digital painting done in Photoshop.

It's wise to take full advantage of the knowledge shared by more experienced artists who have walked this path before. These mentors may be digital or traditional painters, and there is so much to learn from them. But as the saying goes, 'Experience is the lantern that only lights the path of the one who carries it'.

Nothing replaces hands-on practice. There's no better teacher than making mistakes, wrestling with a problem for months, and finally discovering the solution—that kind of growth runs deep. Still, a helping hand can make a world of difference.

FIGURE 0.3 Digital painting done in Photoshop for *Assassin's Creed Valhalla* (*Assassin's Creed* TM & © Ubisoft Entertainment. All Rights Reserved).

The purpose of this book is to be that helping hand—a resource you return to, to find clarity when you need it most. It also aims to answer the questions that many students have when learning digital painting. Often, newcomers chase solutions in the wrong direction, leading to unnecessary frustration. This book is designed to give you those answers *before* discouragement sets in.

The journey to becoming a skilled digital painter is never-ending. Even the most accomplished artists continue to learn throughout their lives. While it may be impossible to know everything, the pursuit of mastery should fill your life with joy and purpose—because your thirst for learning must be boundless.

Give yourself short-, medium-, and long-term goals. In the short term (today to within two years), learn to copy shapes, values, colors, and compositions; understand the fundamentals of painting. In the medium term (2–5 years), be able to produce a solid illustration, on demand, with a design, lighting, and composition that hold up, and this in a reasonable time. In the long term (5–10 years), be a respected and reliable illustrator and/or concept artist, capable of adapting to any style and any context.

FIGURE 0.4 Digital painting done in Photoshop for *Assassin's Creed Unity* (*Assassin's Creed* TM & © Ubisoft Entertainment. All Rights Reserved).

Don't expect to become a master the moment you finish this book—it will take time. This book is here to hold your hand, to keep you from falling and giving up. Think of it like learning to ride a bike: After the training wheels come off, someone still needs to hold the saddle. And yes, once one lets you go, chances are you'll fall. But hopefully you'll come back to this book—again—until the moment you can ride on your own.

Then, you'll be ready to forge your own path, and maybe even become a champion.

If you're already an accomplished artist, thank you sincerely for stopping by—your curiosity and openness speak volumes about your humility. I hope you'll discover a few new ideas within these pages that inspire further exploration and experimentation.

FIGURE 1.1 Digital painting done in Photoshop for *Assassin's Creed Unity* (*Assassin's Creed* TM & © Ubisoft Entertainment. All Rights Reserved).

CHAPTER 1

Material

DOI: 10.1201/9781003536703-2

The choice of equipment often depends on personal preferences and habits. The following information is provided purely for reference.

SOFTWARE

Your primary work tool will probably be Photoshop. It is a perfect tool for creating good digital paintings. Other painting software, such as Artrage, Krita, and Painter, have great qualities, sometimes even superior to Photoshop, especially in simulating traditional painting. However, I found difficult to complete an entire digital painting in any of these softwares, except, of course, for fun or experimentation, which you should do.

FIGURE 1.2 It is good to test other software to paint. Here is one done in Rebelle 3. The simulation of watercolor is very realistic.

As for 3D, it's good to know at least one software, even if it's just in a superficial way. Knowing how to create simple shapes (primitives), navigate with the camera, and do basic lighting may be sufficient. In this book, you will most of the time learn how to use 3D simply as a reference for drawing, especially when it comes to creating a scene with complex architecture that requires drawing complicated shapes in perspective. In this case, a simple screenshot of the 3D is enough. You then put it on a layer in Photoshop in *screen* mode and use it as a guide to paint shapes.

FIGURE 1.3A Here is an example of a simple 3D layout you can use as a drawing reference. No lighting, no textures.

FIGURE 1.3B The same screenshot with a Photoshop filter 'glowing edges' applied on it. Now you can use this image as a drawing, and you can concentrate on the painting. More details on this technique later.

As explained in more detail later, you can sometimes use 3D renders as a base. In those cases, you'll need to invest more time in the 3D setup and then paint over the rendered result in Photoshop. The problem with this method is that you can always feel the look of the 3D in the result, but some Art Directors prefer this kind of image because it is closer to the look of the final product (the video game or the movie).

FIGURE 1.4 Digital matte painting done for an *Assassin's Creed Unity* in-game cinematic (*Assassin's Creed* TM & © Ubisoft Entertainment. All Rights Reserved). It is painted over a 3D render. For this kind of result, you must spend a good amount of time on the 3D scene before starting to paint on it.

As a 3D software, Blender is very popular because it's free (you only pay for the add-ons you need), powerful and user-friendly.

Let's also mention Medium, which is sculpting software that can be used with a virtual reality headset. The latter is fascinating, especially useful for sculpting organic shapes, which are often difficult to achieve with traditional 3D software. The downside with virtual sculpting is that the result always appears better when you have the virtual reality headset on, compared to the actual result, because the immersion aspect disappears. A scene can therefore appear epic when navigated virtually and very ordinary once rendered on a screen.

As for Blender, it is easy to use and very user-friendly. Additionally, you can save a lot of time by purchasing assets or add-ons specific to your needs, often at very reasonable prices. There are also tons of free tutorials available online, making it very accessible even for beginners.

FIGURE 1.5A Here is the interface of Blender.

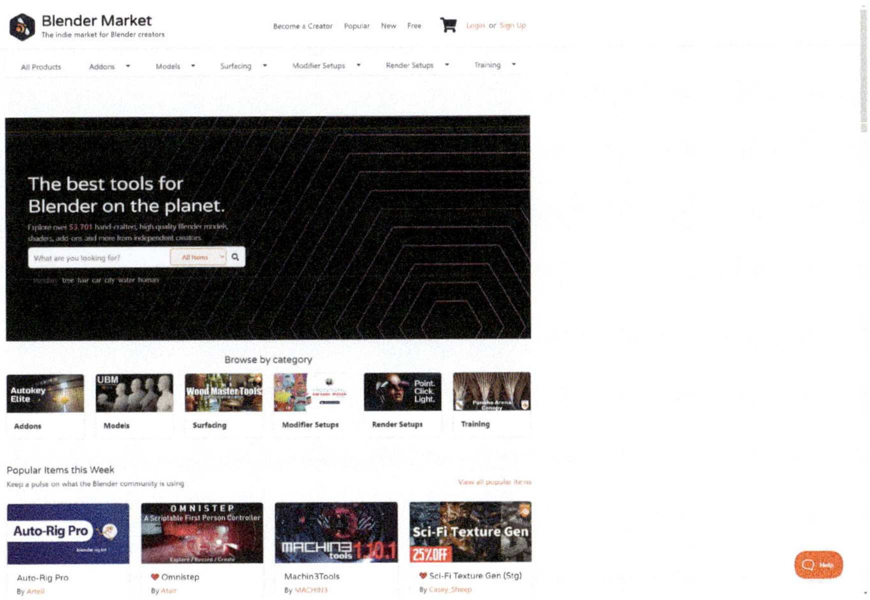

FIGURE 1.5B Home page of Blender Market, where you can purchase add-ons, textures, and models to help with your project.

CINTIQ OR INTUOS?

Wacom products are the most used on the market now, even if other brands exist. You can use both the Cintiq and the Intuos in production, and both have their advantages.

FIGURE 1.5C The Wacom Intuos medium size (photography by Kawê Rodrigues on Unsplash).

First, the Cintiq is a beautiful tool—ideal if your work consists entirely of drawing or sketching. However, if you like to paste reference photos and paint over them, the process can feel a bit clunky on this. You often need to reach for your mouse and keyboard, which can pull you out of your creative bubble and interrupt your flow. Another aspect, even though it may seem strange, is that seeing your hand drawing in front of your canvas can be a bit unsettling, especially when you are used to having your drawing full screen with just the cursor of your brush visible.

FIGURE 1.5D The Wacom Cintiq is fun to work with (photography by Norbert Levajsics on Unsplash).

The last point is more important and concerns the distance you have from your image. On the Cintiq, you tend to focus a lot on the details, and sometimes you may lack perspective. In fact, the quality of your image never depends on the details but on foundations that are much more general.

In conclusion, the ideal setup would be to use both: a Cintiq for the initial sketches, then switch to Intuos to develop most of the image. Finally, you could return to Cintiq to refine details and clean up the shapes. This back-and-forth approach offers the best of both worlds.

That said, some artists work entirely with one or the other—and that's perfectly valid. Ultimately, it's all a matter of personal preference.

SAVE YOUR PREFERRED INTERFACE IN PHOTOSHOP

To be efficient, it's essential to have the right tools and to organize these tools in a way that, while working, you don't have to search for them or even think about them. Navigating through menus and tools should become automatic and natural. You want to be focused on the things that are important for the success of your digital painting, and it's not by spending five minutes looking for a particular menu. Therefore, try to organize your interface in your own way so that your work is as efficient and smooth as possible. Here is a suggestion for the Photoshop interface:

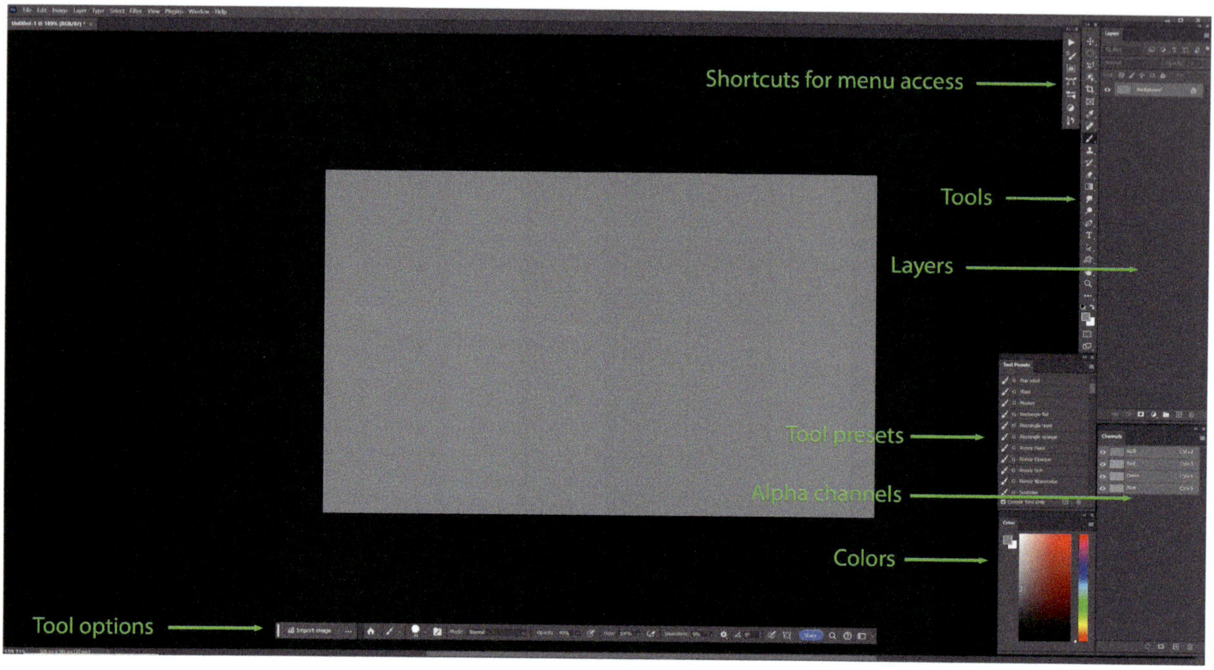

FIGURE 1.6A Notice how most menus are positioned on the right side—making this setup more suitable for right-handed users.

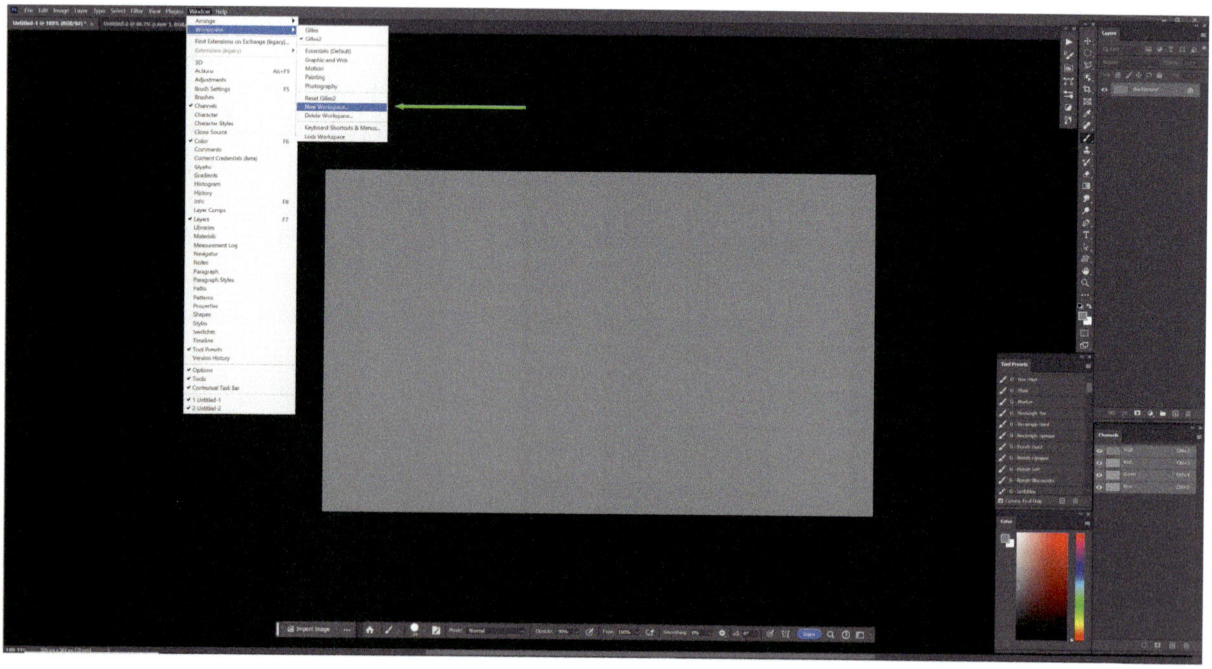

FIGURE 1.6B Save your interface through the menu: Window/Workspace/New Workspace.

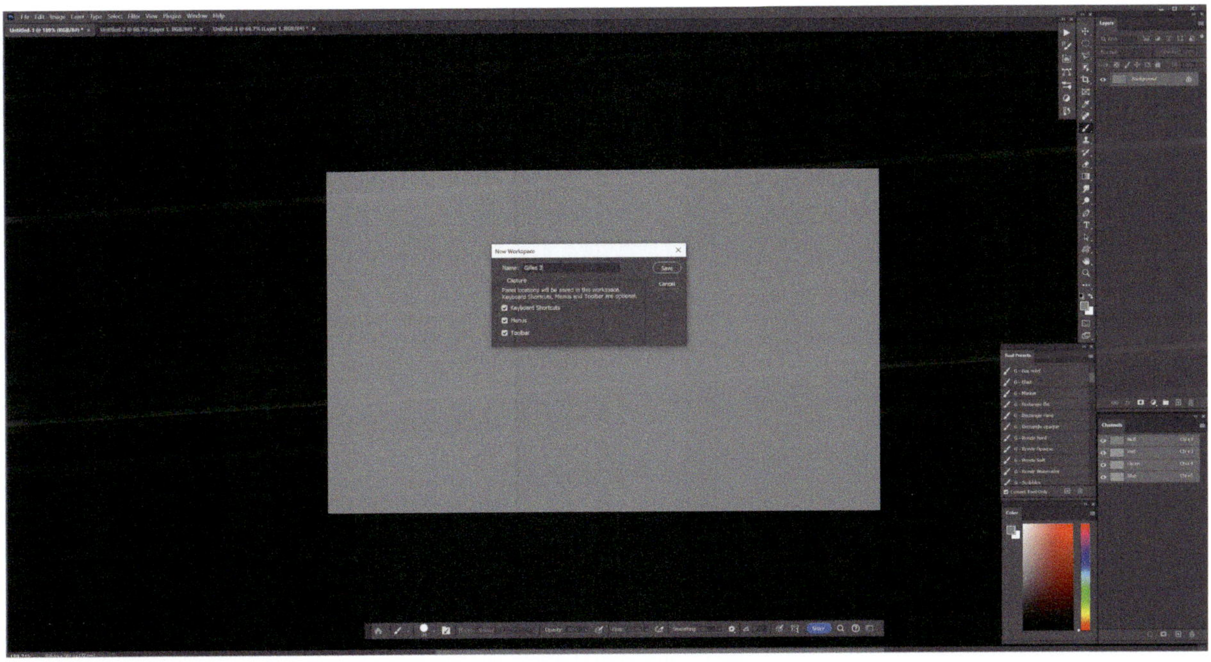

FIGURE 1.6C Name your workspace, check all the boxes and click 'Save'.

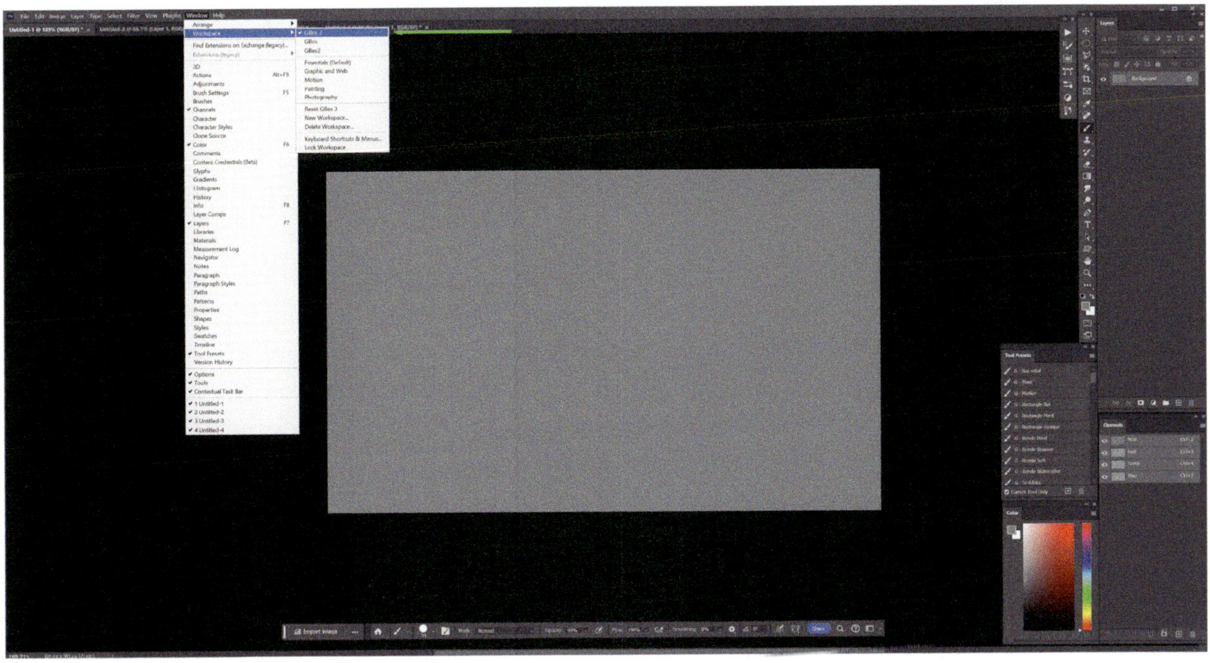

FIGURE 1.6D Now you can find your saved workspace in Window/Workspace.

SHORTCUTS

You will probably use a lot of shortcuts in Photoshop, and you can customize some of them to make the work process faster and easier. You can set up them in the menu *Edit/Keyboard shortcuts.*

FIGURE 1.7 You can find the keyboard shortcuts menu in Edit/Keyboard Shortcuts.

SELECT YOUR BRUSHES

Discovering new brushes that you like is always an exciting moment. You think you've finally found something that will truly change your way of working, and it's true that the choice of brushes can radically influence the style of your digital painting.

You might test many of them and have hundreds in reserve. However, you'll probably realize that after a while, you always end up working with only about a dozen of them, and always the same ones. Here are a bunch of important ones:

FIGURE 1.8 The round brush with a watercolor feel.

The first one is a round brush with variable opacity, which can be called *the watercolor round,* because its transparency resembles that medium. It's a brush that comes by default in Photoshop. Very useful for painting any shape and texture. A must-have.

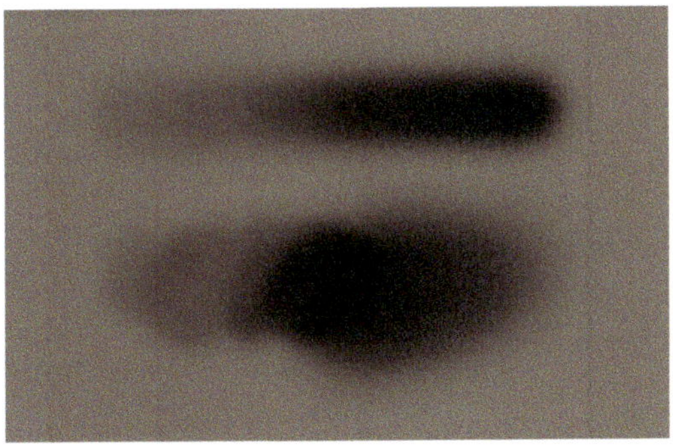

FIGURE 1.9 The airbrush.

The second one is the airbrush, which is very useful for softening an edge, reducing contrast, adding a contact shadow or some fog. You can also paint entire sections just with this brush in places where you don't want any hard edges. However, be careful not to overuse it and counterbalance with sharper zones, as the result could appear blurry and amateurish.

FIGURE 1.10 Different opaque brushes that help to paint precise silhouettes.

The third type of brush you should try is of various shapes and with 100% opacity. These allow you to paint shapes and silhouettes precisely.

FIGURE 1.11 Various brushes a bit more random in terms of shapes. Helpful to get some 'happy accidents'.

Keep one or two brushes for sketching. They will have variable shapes depending on the angle of the stroke, which will create a bit of chaos and happy accidents, which are useful when sketching quickly.

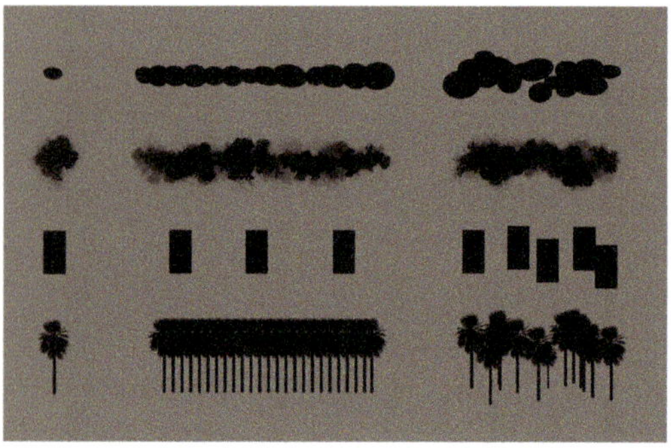

FIGURE 1.12 Examples of various brushes that allow you to get some illusion of details or texture very fast.

Occasionally, you may use other types of brushes for specific needs. For example, painting the silhouette of a leafy tree, blades of grass, or adding texture to an object. This will be especially in cases where you need to be very precise or sketch an idea quickly.

CUSTOM BRUSHES

You can create your own brushes if you like. It can be very useful, for example, when working on a cartoon-style project. Some shapes can be recurring.

Here's the procedure to customize your brush:

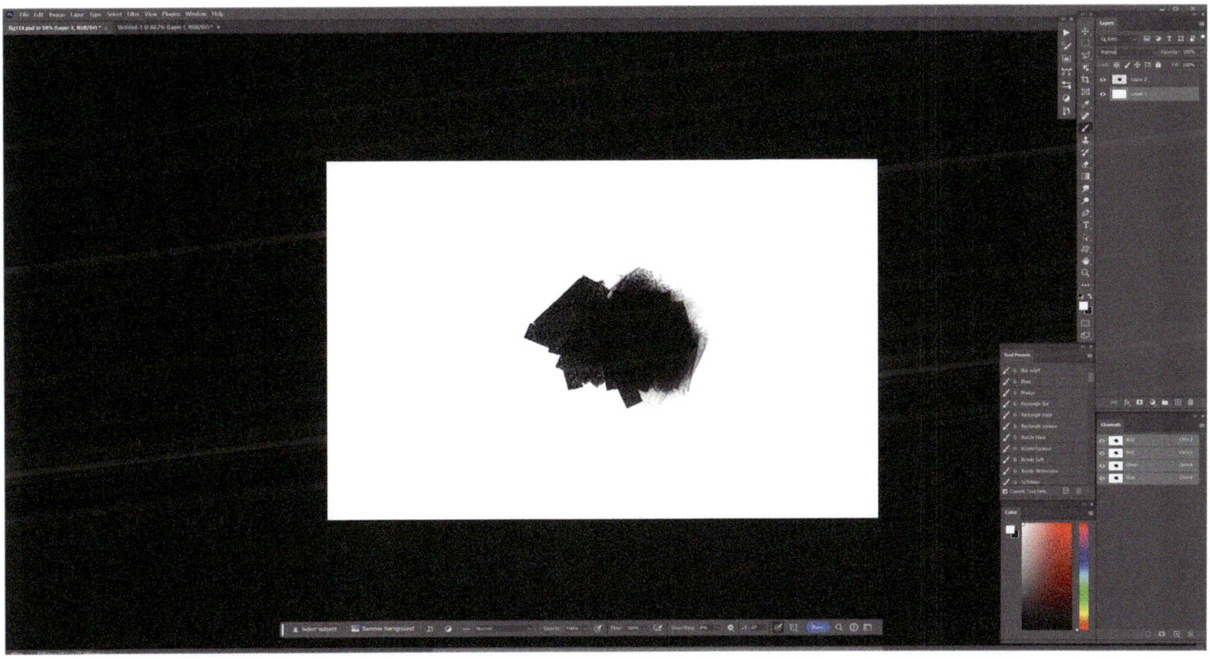

FIGURE 1.13A First, create a black shape on a white canvas. You can paint it, scan it, or create it with shapes. The important thing is that the result must be the main shape you want your brush to resemble.

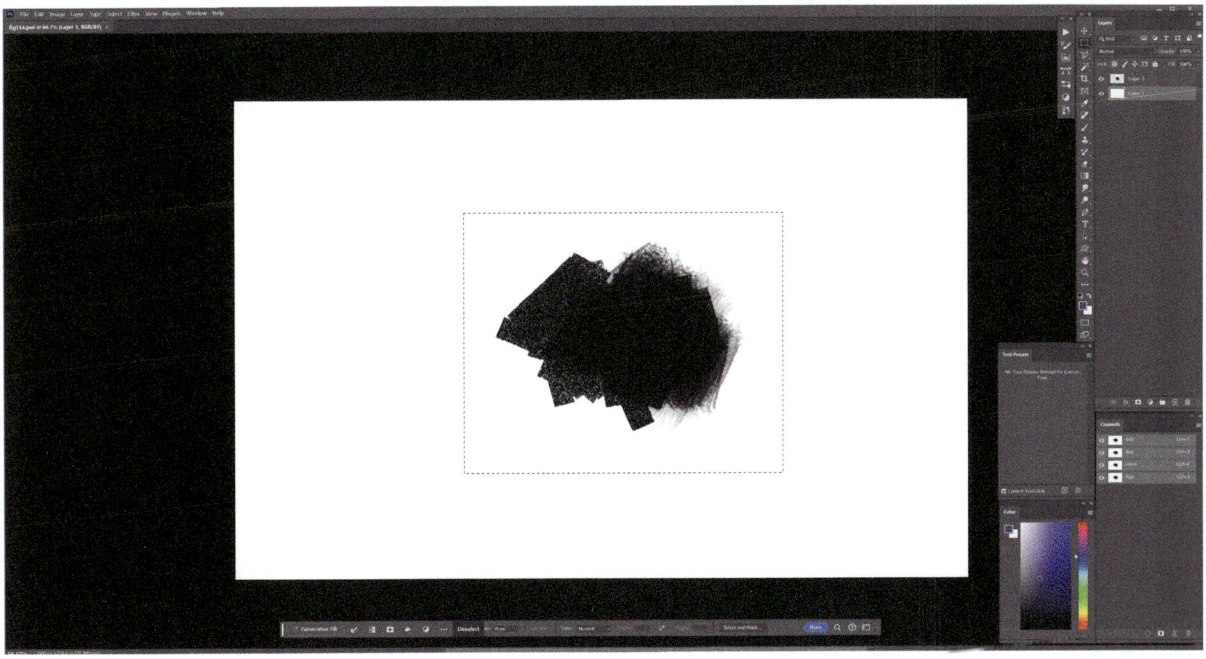

FIGURE 1.13B Then, select the area you want to define as your brush. Black will be 100% opaque; white will be transparent.

FIGURE 1.13C Click on *'Edit/Define Brush Preset'*.

FIGURE 1.13D Name your brush, click 'OK'.

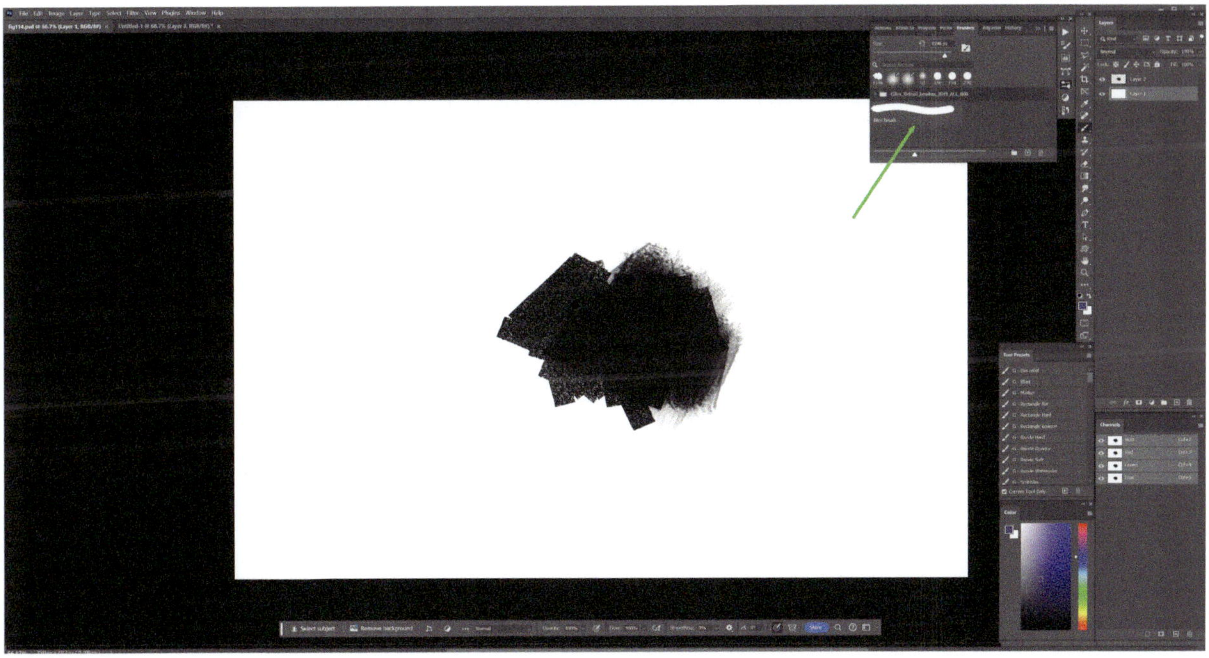

FIGURE 1.13E You can see your brush saved here.

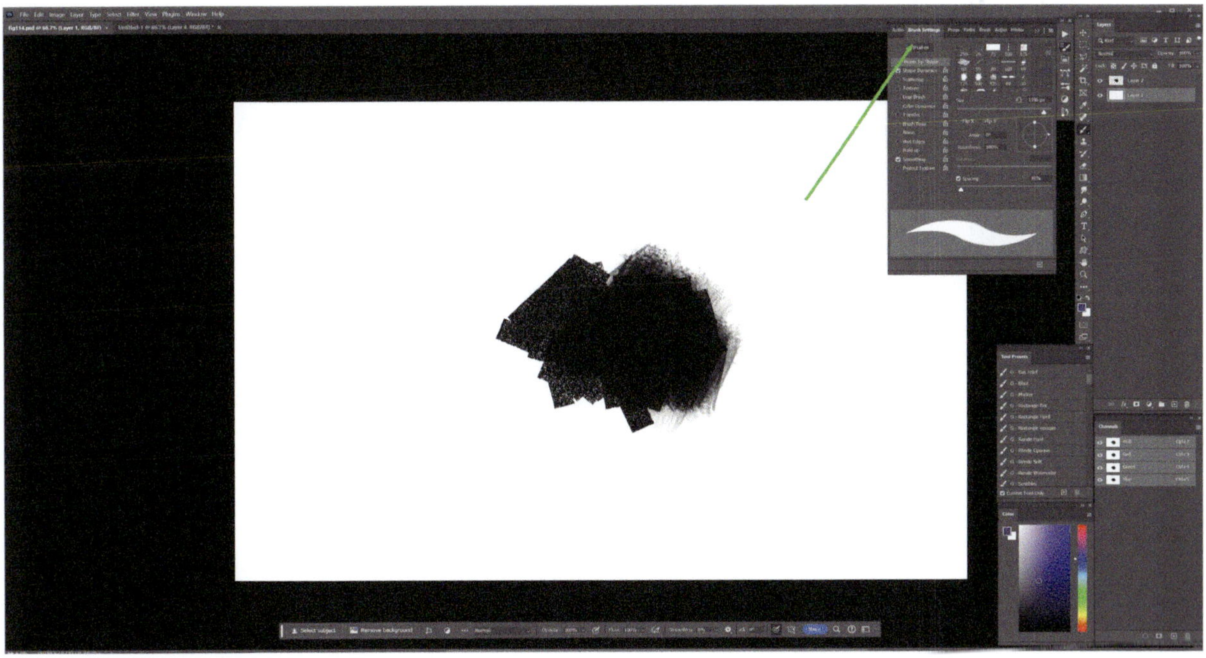

FIGURE 1.13F Now go to the brush settings menu.

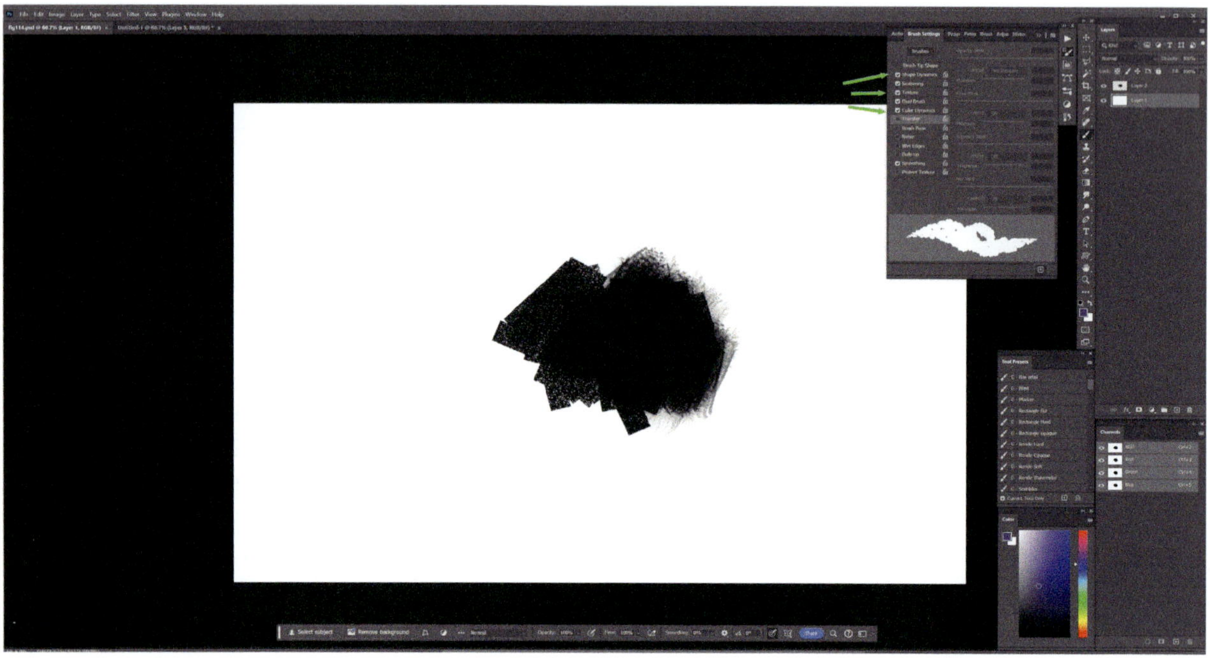

FIGURE 1.13G Have fun playing and testing the different settings to get the result you want.

FIGURE 1.13H Click on the '+' and name your brush with its new settings.

FIGURE 1.131 Your new brush appears here; you can now delete the first one. That's it!

CUSTOM SHAPES

This tool is great not only for graphic designers. It is also extremely useful to paint digitally. The reasoning behind this need is as follows: First, focus on the outer shape of what you are painting, let's say the silhouette, and then paint inside that shape. The result is precise, and the execution is very fast. Let's take the example of a forest in the background that you must paint: You can use several custom tree shapes to create the silhouette and then use that silhouette as a selection to paint inside. It's extremely efficient.

FIGURE 1.14A Pick the Custom Shape Tool and create a new layer.

FIGURE 1.14B Right click and pick the custom shape you need.

FIGURE 1.14C Use your custom shapes to get a nice silhouette.

FIGURE 1.14D CTRL left click on the layer to get your shape as a selection.

FIGURE 1.14E Delete the layer and create a new one.

FIGURE 1.14F Hide the selection (CTRL+H) and paint inside your shape. Now you get an interesting and clean silhouette.

MAKE YOUR OWN CUSTOM SHAPE

As you see, it is efficient. Now, here is how to create your own custom shape:

FIGURE 1.15A First, paint a shape or pick a photo with a shape you can extract from. Be aware that the resolution of your image will be the resolution of your custom shape. If it's too big, it might slow down the performance of Photoshop. So, adjust the resolution accordingly.

FIGURE 1.15B You need to get rid of the colors. You can desaturate the image with Image/Adjustments/Hue-Saturation.

FIGURE 1.15C Use Image/Adjustments/Levels to have only 2 values left (black and white).

FIGURE 1.15D Clean the silhouette as much as possible with an opaque brush and then select the black part with select/color range.

FIGURE 1.15E In window/path, click on 'Make Work Path' to transform your selection as a path.

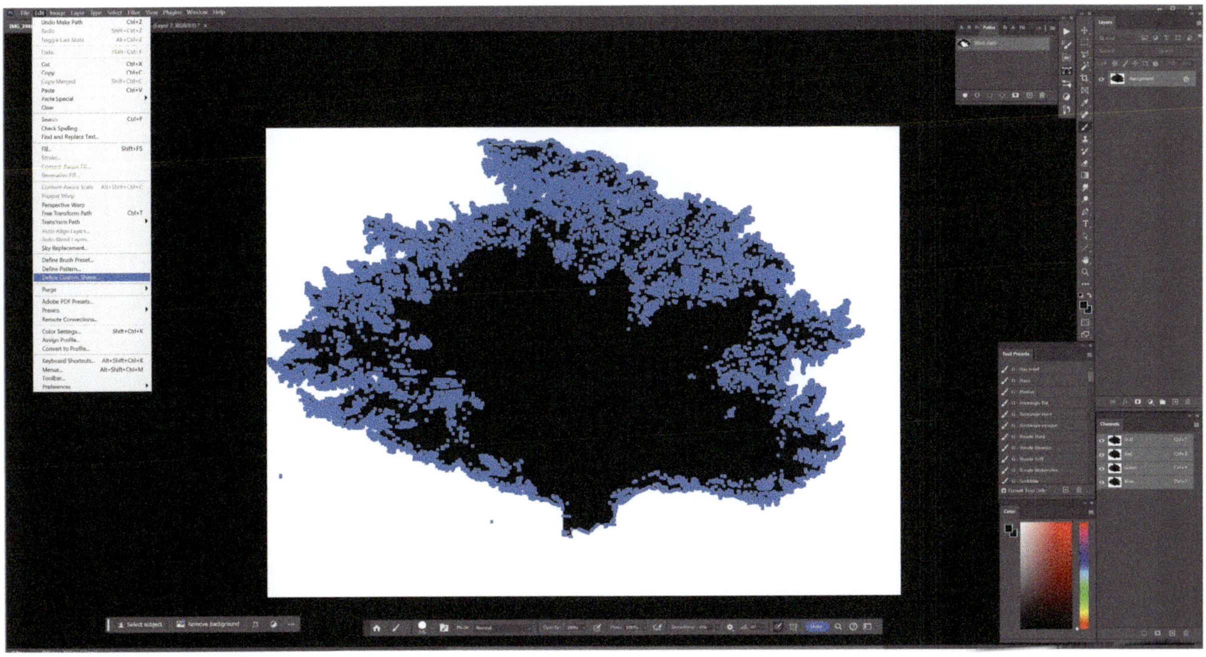

FIGURE 1.15F It should now look like this. Go to Edit/Define Custom Shape.

FIGURE 1.15G You can name your new custom shape.

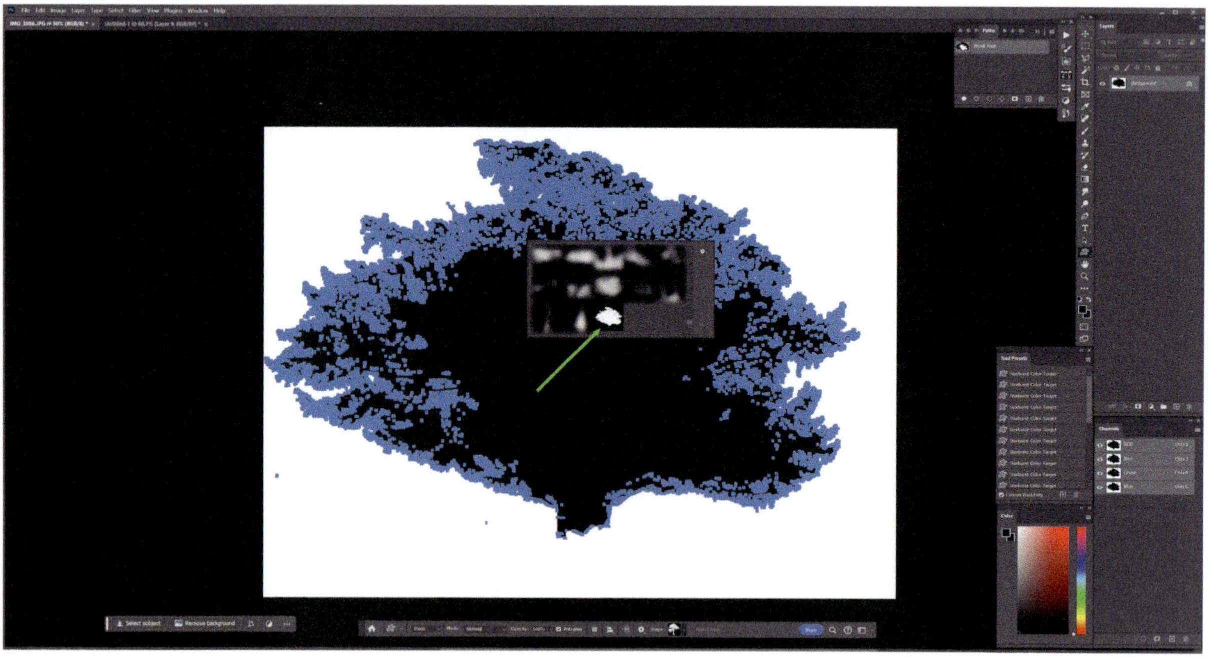

FIGURE 1.15H Pick the Custom shape tool and Right Click, you should see your new custom shape listed.

FIGURE 1.15I You can now use your new Custom Shape.

MIXER BRUSH

The mixer brush is a great tool as well. The principle is that instead of picking up a color from your painting with the dropper, you pick up a small part of the image (or from another image), which then becomes your 'paint'. The result then varies depending on the mixer brush shape and settings you use, and the results can be very surprising. It's useful when you need to convey texture in your brushstrokes, or when you want to add volume, such as painting a cable or a building very quickly. Test it out to see the full potential and how you can use it.

FIGURE 1.16A Select the Mixer brush tool. Pick from a photo reference (Ctrl on your keyboard) with the desired texture, choose your brush shape (right-click), and start painting. Pick from the shadow areas to get shadow values and from the light areas to get light values. The results can be very surprising!

FIGURE 1.16B The photo reference is on the left. You can see the interesting results you can get. Note that you need to use the same settings visible on the toolbar and select a similar brush shape to achieve the same result.

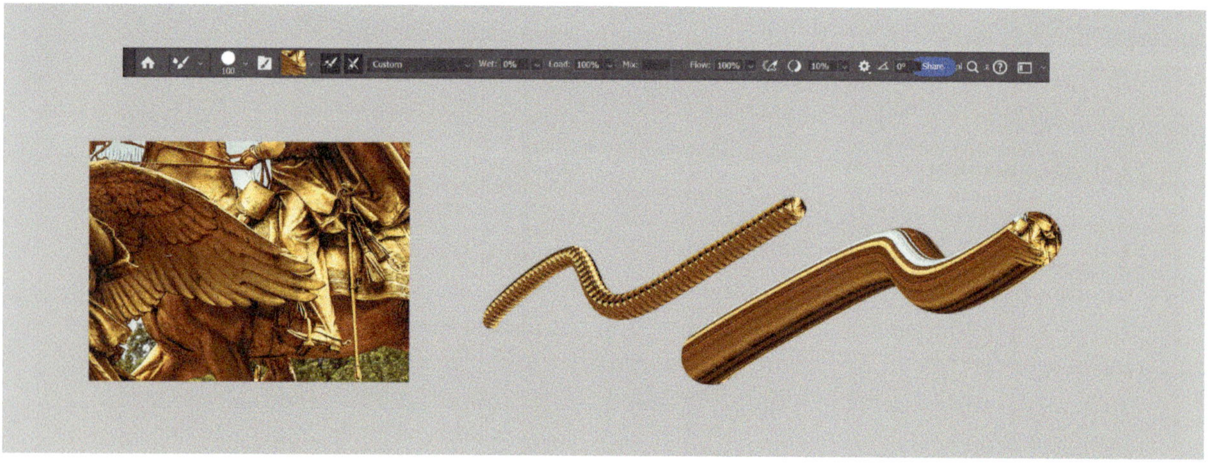

FIGURE 1.16C Selecting the same image but using different brush shapes can result in significantly different brushstroke qualities. First, brushstrokes were done with an opaque round mixer brush, then with the watercolor round. The results vary slightly, making this technique particularly useful for quickly painting ropes or cables.

In conclusion, the Mixer Brush is fun to paint with and can be very useful, especially for quickly creating textures or shapes.

USE AND SAVE YOUR SELECTIONS

To save you time, save all the selections you use so you can quickly retrieve them when needed. There's nothing more frustrating than having to redo a selection that you forgot to save. There are several ways to proceed:

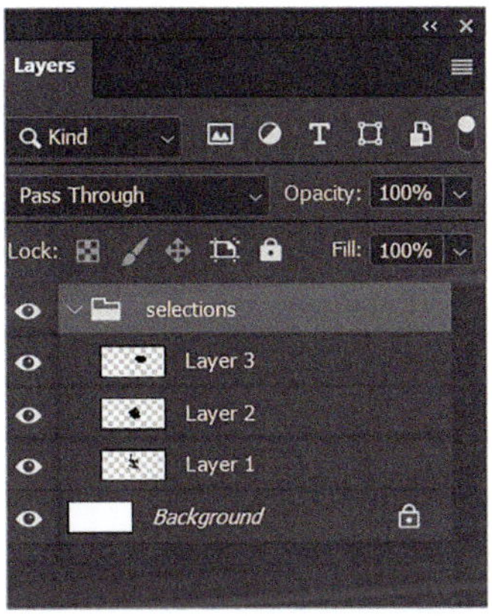

FIGURE 1.17 Here is an example of how you can save your selections by placing your opaque shapes on layers within a dedicated group.

First, you can keep your opaque shapes on layers that you stack in a 'selection' folder.

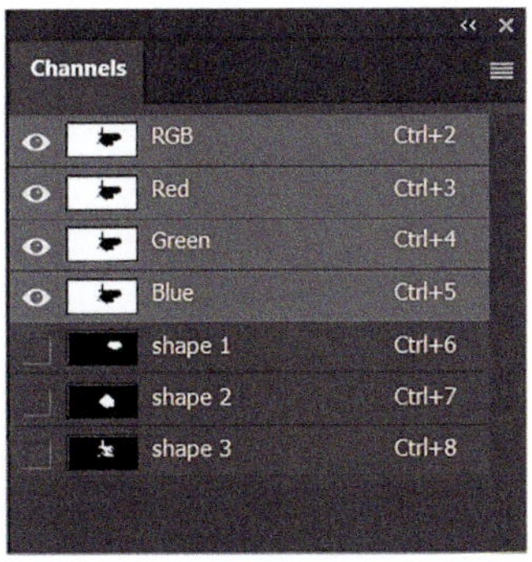

FIGURE 1.18 You can save your selections as Alpha channels and name them.

Or keep your selections in the *channels* section.

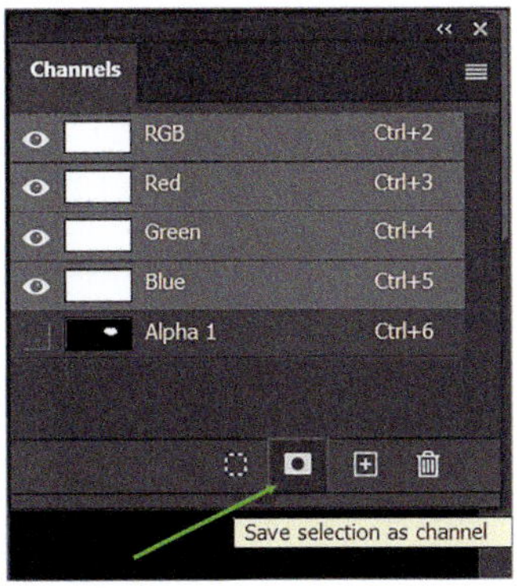

FIGURE 1.19 After defining your selection in your painting, click on this icon to save your selection as an Alpha channel. The first selection will appear as 'Alpha 1'. You can rename it if needed.

If you save your selections as alpha channels, keep that section visible beneath your layers for quick access (see Figure 1.6a). This layout makes navigation much more intuitive. The only downside is that storing many selections can noticeably increase the size of your Photoshop file. To prevent this, regularly clean up your alpha channels and keep only the selections that are still relevant.

THE CURVE TOOL

This tool is essential for digital painting—and it's likely one of the main reasons artists find it hard to let go of Photoshop in favor of other software. It allows you to adjust lighting, values, and color temperatures with precision. Not only is it comprehensive and user-friendly, but it also offers powerful flexibility: You can apply adjustments to the entire image or use a mask to affect only specific areas, painting in exactly what you want to reveal.

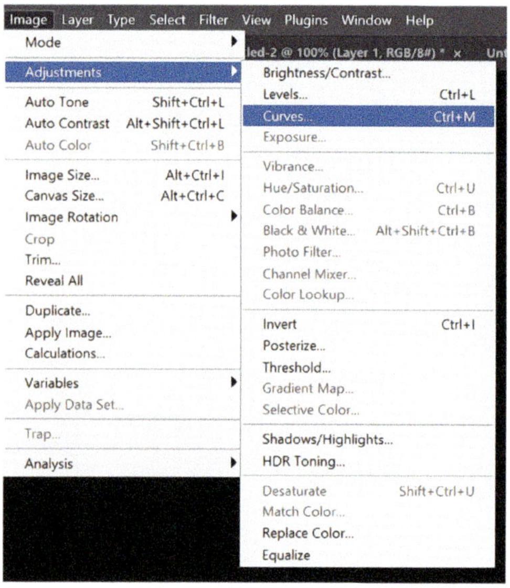

FIGURE 1.20A You can find the Curves adjustments tool in Image/Adjustments/Curves.

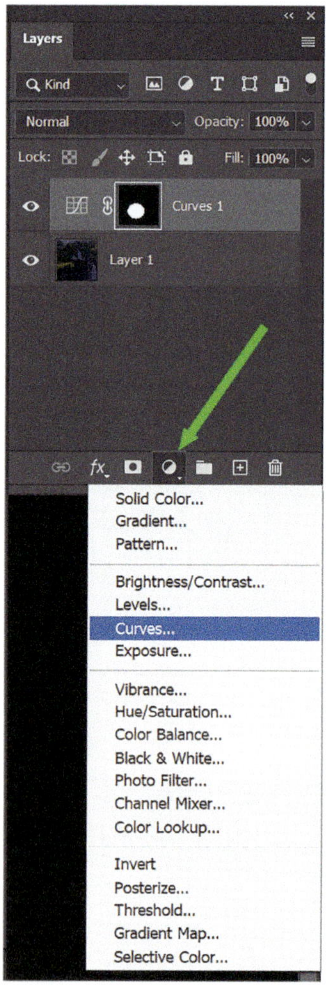

FIGURE 1.20B You can also add a Curves adjustment layer by clicking here. In this example, the effects of the curves tool will affect only the part inside a circle painted on the mask.

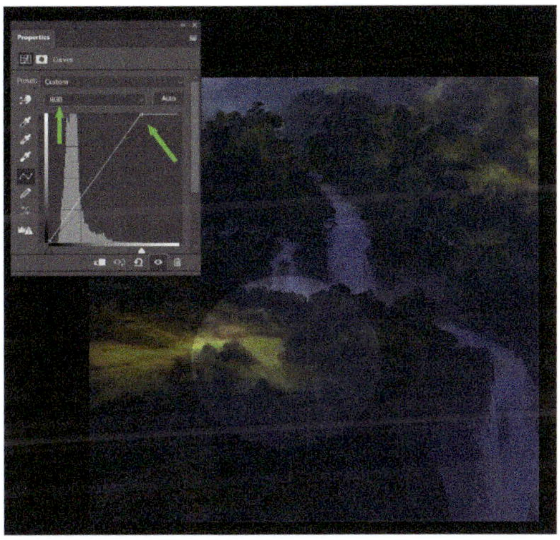

FIGURE 1.20C In the Curves tool menu, if you select RGB and move this point toward the top left, you'll see the lighter values go lighter.

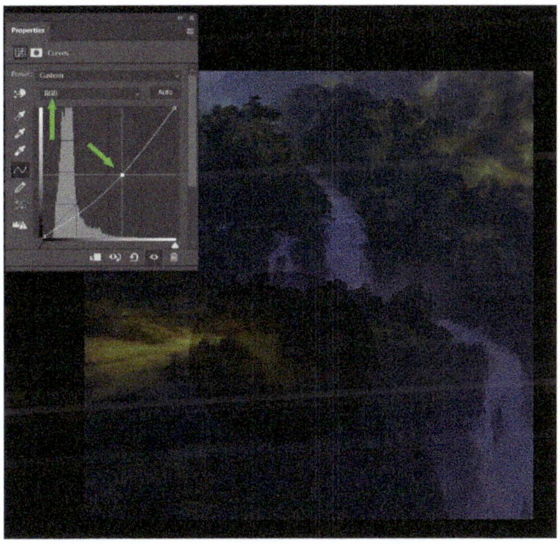

FIGURE 1.20D If you still select RGB and move the middle values point toward the bottom right, the middle values of your painting will be darker.

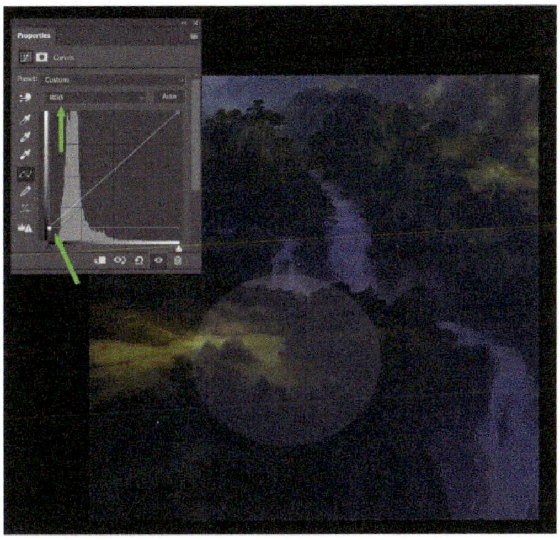

FIGURE 1.20E If you move the dark values point toward the top, those values will become lighter.

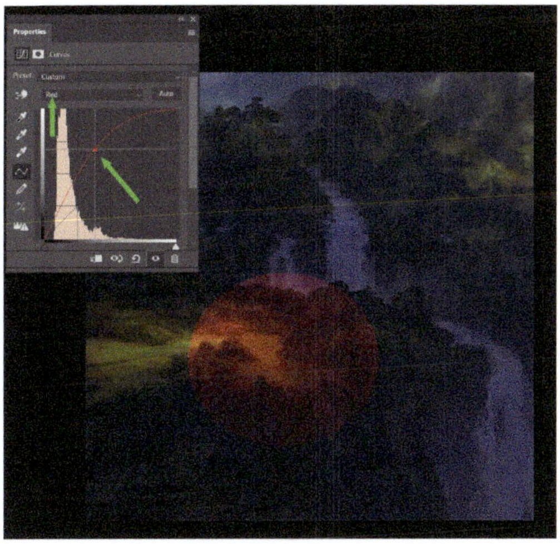

FIGURE 1.20F This time, if you select the red channel and move the mid values point to the top left, you'll see the colors shifting to red.

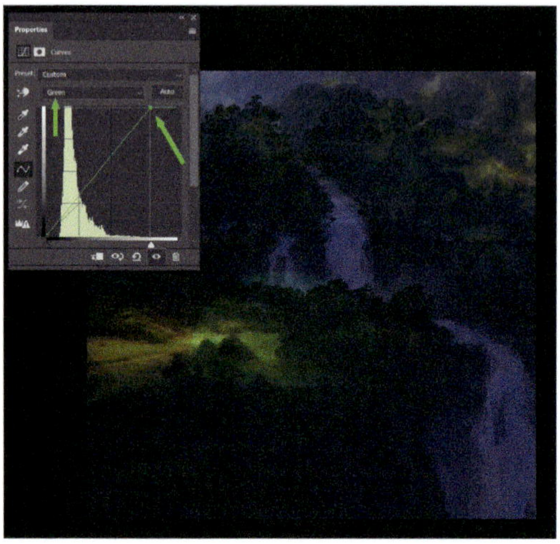

FIGURE 1.20G Now, if you select the green channel and move the high values point to the top left, you'll see the high values colors shifting to green.

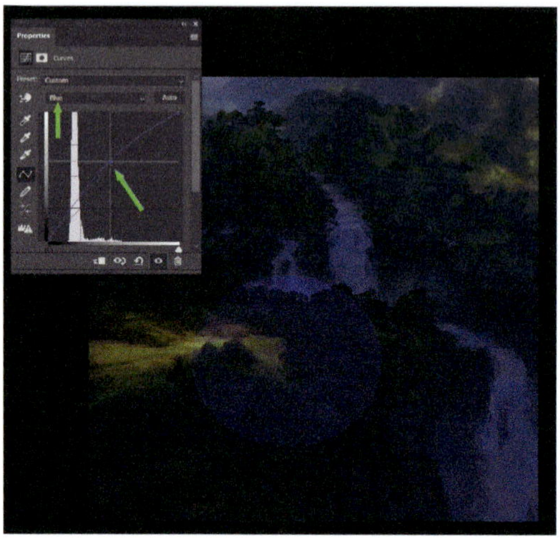

FIGURE 1.20H Then, if you select the blue channel and move the mid values point to the top left, you'll see the mid values colors shifting to blue, and so on.

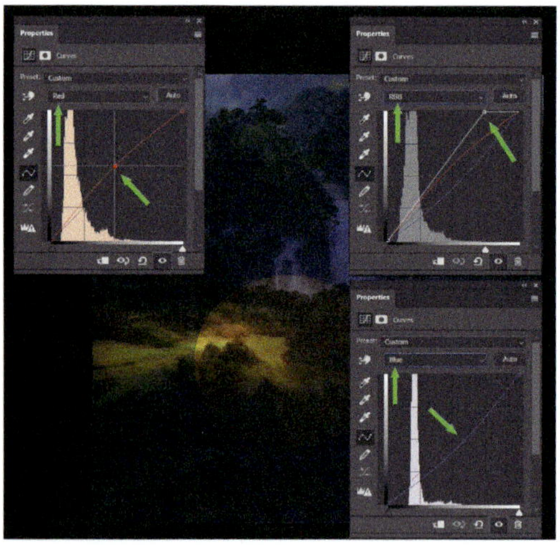

FIGURE 1.20I Of course, you can combine Curves adjustments. Here, you can add more red, less blue (so more yellow), and lighten the values. You may add a bright, warm light by painting on the mask in the area that needs to be lightened. You can use this method very often to add light and play with variations of color temperatures.

FIGURE 2.1 Digital painting done in Photoshop for *Assassin's Creed Unity* (*Assassin's Creed* TM & © Ubisoft Entertainment. All Rights Reserved).

CHAPTER 2

Composition

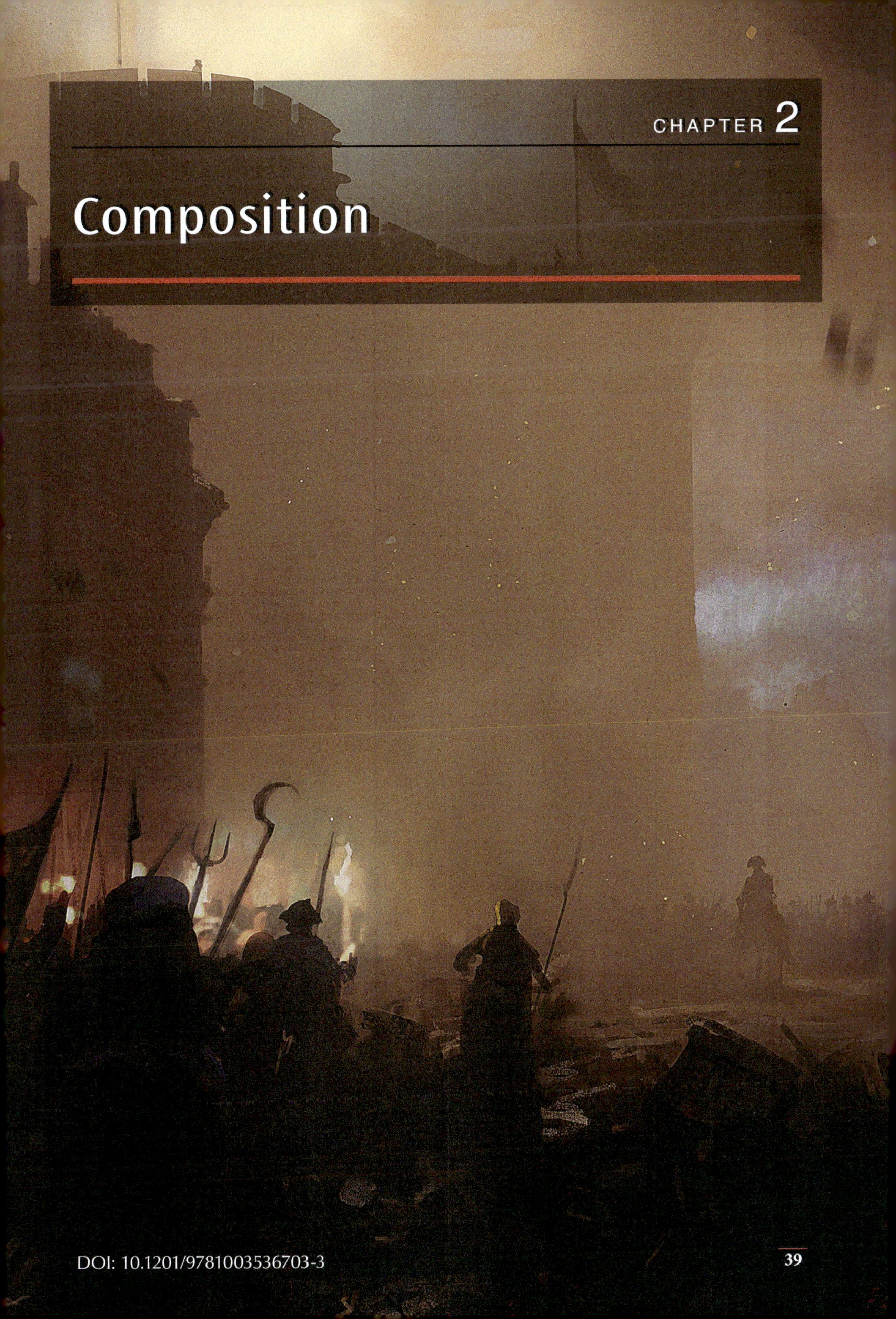

DOI: 10.1201/9781003536703-3

Before listing some helpful image composition rules, it's important to note that if your digital painting looks great without following any of them—that's perfectly fine! Rules of composition exist to help you when your image doesn't seem to work at this level. If you feel that your eye doesn't stop at your focal point from the first seconds and takes a bit of time to find out where to look and what to look at. In that case, go back to these rules and see how you could improve things. On the other hand, if you find an interesting and readable composition despite breaking these rules, it means you probably have a digital painting that stands out and will catch attention. But it must be admitted that it's rare. These rules are, of course, not dogmatic; they exist because they come from centuries of practice in the art of storytelling through images, and artists know what pleases the human eye and what is difficult to read. In conclusion, don't blindly follow these rules; it's just good to know them and revisit them when needed. However, when you paint, you should go with your feelings first. If you find that your composition works, it's probably enough.

FIGURE 2.2 Digital painting done in Photoshop for *Assassin's Creed Valhalla* (*Assassin's Creed* TM & © Ubisoft Entertainment. All Rights Reserved)

IMPORTANCE OF CONTRAST

It's an important concept, and it pertains to several chapters of this book. The concept of contrast is extremely important when creating an illustration, as it makes your image more interesting to look at. What exactly does it entail? It turns out that the person viewing your image enjoys being entertained. They like being able to compare the different aspects of your painting with one another. The more contrasts there are, the more the person will enjoy spending time looking at your image. And this notion of contrast can apply to everything: objects, distances, scale, colors, values, design, and more. For instance, to make an object look very large, you can place other objects beside it that look very tiny in comparison. If you want to show that something is more colorful, the rest should be more desaturated, and so on. The applications are nearly infinite! Near/far contrasts, warm/cold, busy/calm, full/empty, alone/in a group, heavy/light, big/small, dark/light, textured/smooth, in motion/stationary, beautiful/ugly, violent/peaceful, and so on. Playing with two complementary colors also falls into this category. A character dressed in red in a lush green landscape will provide an interesting contrast. Try to think about playing with this notion of contrast, and your digital painting will only benefit from it.

FIGURE 2.3 A lot of different contrasts in this digital painting: far/close, warm/cool, light/dark, alone/many, dull/saturated, in movement/still, etc. Note how a basic 'rule' of composition is broken here: The main value contrast lies in a corner of the image (digital painting done in Photoshop for *For Honor*, © Ubisoft Entertainment. All Rights Reserved).

FOREGROUND, MIDGROUND, BACKGROUND

This is a classic element of a successful composition. This is not a rule, and don't hesitate to play around with this concept. However, in your ongoing effort to create an illusion of depth in your images, and also to add a type of contrast (in this case, the contrast of near/far), clearly establishing objects in the foreground, midground and background will be one of the techniques used to give the illusion of a three-dimensional environment while working with a two-dimensional medium. If you feel that your image appears flat, clearly defining these three planes is a first step that can help. This way, the viewer will find it easier to read your painting and, therefore, to immerse themselves in it.

FIGURE 2.4 A clear front, middle and background in this digital painting done in Photoshop for *Assassin's Creed Unity* (*Assassin's Creed* TM & © Ubisoft Entertainment. All Rights Reserved).

FOCUS POINT

A focal point is the area of your image that should be the first thing the viewer looks at in your painting. It's the number one point of interest. It's crucial that this focal point be decided by you and not left to chance. Nothing is more likely to lose someone's attention than presenting them with an image where they're not sure where to focus.

FIGURE 2.5 Here, the focus points (the character and the eagle) are clear and easy to read (digital painting done in Photoshop for *Assassin's Creed Unity* (*Assassin's Creed* TM & © Ubisoft Entertainment. All Rights Reserved).

This focal point is often a character or an important location in a landscape. If it's a portrait, naturally the focus will be on the subject's eyes. There can be multiple focal points, but most of the time, try not to choose more than three.

FIGURE 2.6 Most of the time, the eyes are the focus point in a portrait painting (study after John Singer Sargent's painting, done in Procreate on iPad Pro).

Typically, there will be one main focal point and one or two secondary ones. You then ensure that there's enough contrast in values and/or colors at these points, as well as a bit more detail. Make sure also not having them too far apart or too close together.

FIGURE 2.7 The eagle, the assassin and the soldier are the three points of interest (digital painting done in Photoshop for *Assassin's Creed Unity* (*Assassin's Creed* TM & © Ubisoft Entertainment. All Rights Reserved).

You also want strong lines (see elsewhere) to guide the viewer's eye towards these focal points, so the image is pleasing to look at and its reading flows easily. You should avoid placing these focal points too close to the edges of the image.

FIGURE 2.8 The church and the character are the main points of interest. Note the guiding lines that lead the eye toward them (digital painting done in Photoshop for *Assassin's Creed Valhalla* (*Assassin's Creed* TM & © Ubisoft Entertainment. All Rights Reserved).

Choosing to follow the rule of thirds (see page 53) to place them is a good starting point. Afterward, of course, you can play around with this, for example, by having strong contrasts elsewhere in the image that compete with a more natural focal point (such as a character's face, for example).

Of course, you should be aware that you're playing with 'rules' that work well, and the result can become unreadable if you completely ignore them. It's up to you to play with these rules, keeping them in mind to understand that you're on treacherous ground, but the result can be very interesting and truly extraordinary if you consciously work around them.

FIGURE 2.9 Observe all the strong lines guiding to the focal point, which is the character (digital painting done in Photoshop for *Assassin's Creed Valhalla* (*Assassin's Creed* TM & © Ubisoft Entertainment. All Rights Reserved).

STORYTELLING

Even if it's not part of your mandate or your Art Director or client hasn't specifically requested it, it's always a good idea to tell a story in your painting, even if the story seems insignificant.

FIGURE 2.10 The goal of this concept was to show how the environment would look, but adding characters into the context introduces a bit of storytelling. It makes the painting more interesting to look at (digital painting done in Photoshop for *For Honor* (© Ubisoft Entertainment. All Rights Reserved).

First, this provides an excuse to integrate characters in an interesting way, which helps to convey the scale of the environment, a very important aspect.

Second, it can be a great source of inspiration for the various teams working on the project. Your image can serve purposes beyond artistic direction. For example, it might inspire a new mission in the game, introduce a gameplay idea, add a storyline, or even a new skill for the main character. It could also help deepen the personality of a character. Whenever you add storytelling elements, they are always greatly appreciated by the team because they can spark many new ideas, some of which you didn't even consider while creating the concept art.

FIGURE 2.11 Even for designing interiors, it's good to have a bit of storytelling. It helps to interest the viewer a bit longer (digital painting done for *Assassin's Creed Unity* (*Assassin's Creed* TM & © Ubisoft Entertainment. All Rights Reserved).

Finally, another advantage is that your image becomes more interesting to look at. The viewer enjoys spending time with it and might even use it as their computer wallpaper for inspiration, which, for a concept artist on a project, is the equivalent of a medal.

In summary, always try to add storytelling; it only brings positive results.

FIGURE 2.12 Many little stories are happening in this painting, even though the goal was to show how this environment should look in the game. (Digital painting done for *Assassin's Creed Revelations* (*Assassin's Creed* TM & © Ubisoft Entertainment. All Rights Reserved).

CLASSICAL COMPOSITION RULES

You have probably already heard about the golden ratio. This method of composing an image can be very effective. It mimics patterns and proportions found in nature. It seems that organic elements form with a certain harmonious logic. These rules are often used in architectural creations and, of course, can also be found in classical paintings. If you follow these rules, there's a good chance your composition will be very pleasing to the eye and appear harmonious.

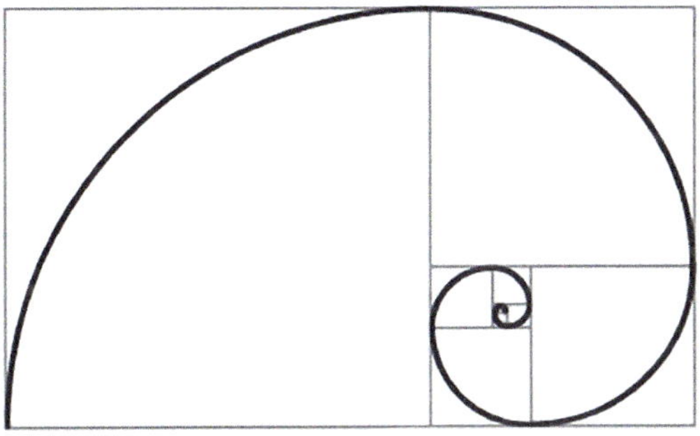

FIGURE 2.13A The golden ratio. Just so you know: In mathematics, two quantities are in the golden ratio if their ratio is the same as the ratio of their sum to the larger of the two quantities. The Greek letter phi (φ or ϕ) denotes the golden ratio. $\varphi = 1.618033$.

FIGURE 2.13B The golden ratio is called the divine proportion because it seems to reflect the logical design behind creation in nature (photography by Megs Harrison on Unsplash).

FIGURE 2.13C Many artists, photographers and architects throughout history have used this divine proportion to make their creations look harmonious. Here is an example of a painting where the use of the golden ratio seems obvious: *The Great Wave off Kanagawa* (1829) by Katsushika Hokusai (1760–1849).

You can also play with the proportions of the image frame and ensure that the strong lines in your painting follow certain lines created from these proportions. You can try to push this concept in a digital painting, and you'll see that the result is indeed interesting.

FIGURE 2.14A The four edges of the frame are the lines you must always deal with, as well as the proportions between the height and the width (digital painting done for *Assassin's Creed Brotherhood* (*Assassin's Creed* TM & © Ubisoft Entertainment. All Rights Reserved).

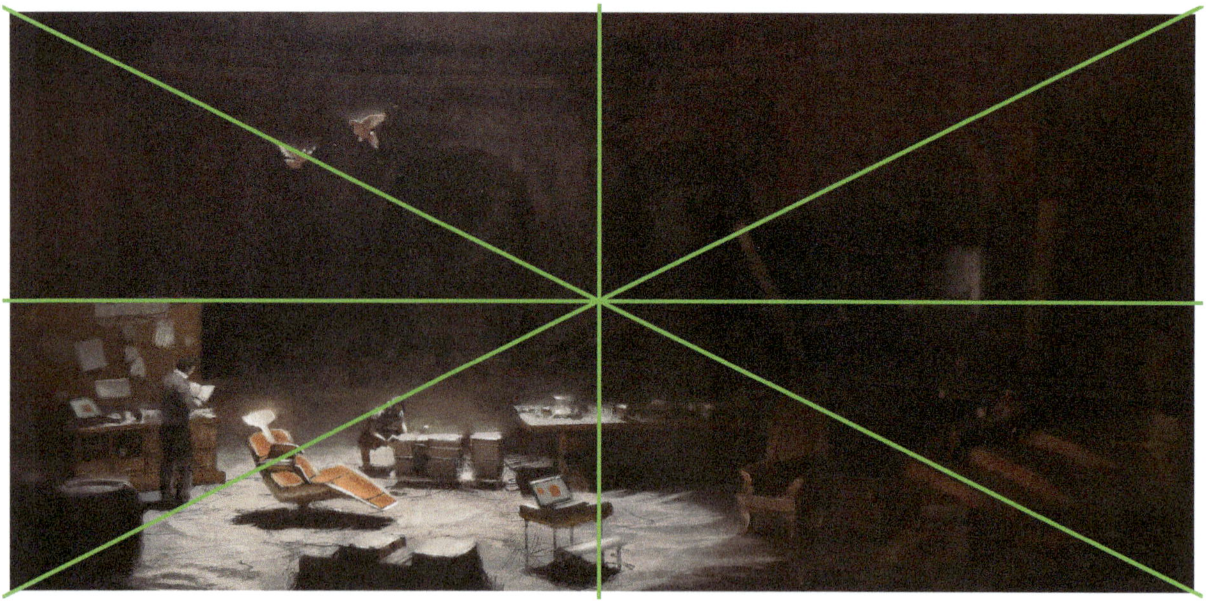

FIGURE 2.14B The diagonals and the lines formed by joining the centers of each edge create strong lines that are indeed in harmony with the proportions of the image.

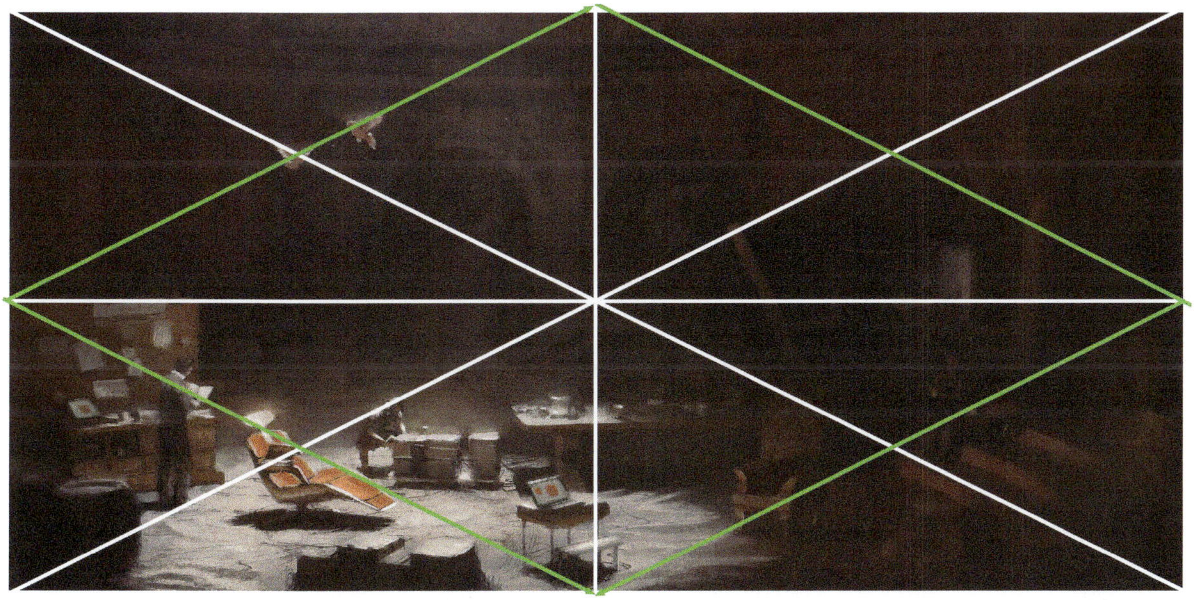

FIGURE 2.14C You can now join the centers of each border in this way. It creates other strong lines.

FIGURE 2.14D You can now draw lines through the centers of those four rectangles formed by the lines drawn before.

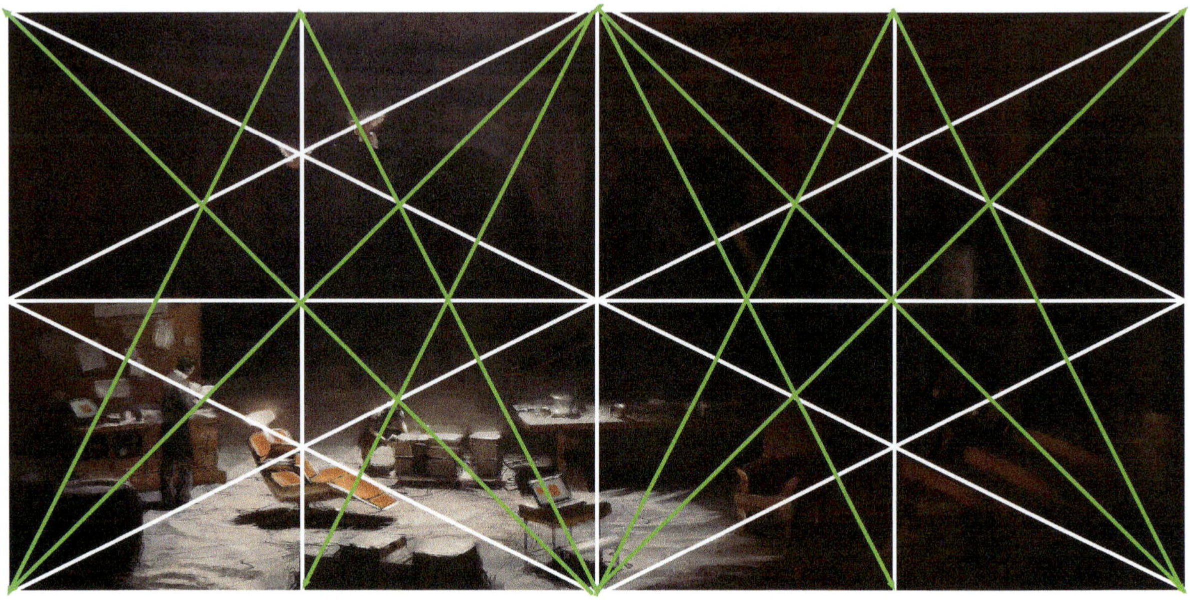

FIGURE 2.14E You can now draw lines that join different points. The number of possibilities is infinite. All these lines are in harmony with the proportions of your image.

FIGURE 2.14F Here the challenge was to follow this composition guide as much as possible to see how it could affect the result. It certainly gives something different and harmonious. Note how the points of interest are where a lot of strong lines meet the most, and the important lines of this digital painting are following some guiding lines. Even the birds' poses follow those guides. It is a very interesting exercise you can test, and keep those guides in mind in your future paintings.

FIGURE 2.15 A good example of the use of the rule of thirds in a composition (photo by Jairph on Unsplash).

RULE OF THIRDS

This is probably the most well-known and widely used composition 'rule'. For the few of you who may not be familiar with it yet, it involves placing your points of interest and strong lines (such as the horizon, for example) on one-third of the length or height of the image. In fact, you just need to divide your image into three equal parts in width and height and place the strong lines of your composition on these lines or place the focus points at the intersections of these lines.

But why does this 'rule' seem to work most of the time? There are two reasons. The first is that placing a focus point or a strong line near the center of the image has a very powerful effect on the viewer (Do you remember the two little girls at the end of the hallway in *The Shining*? See Figure 2.16). It should be used in certain very specific situations; otherwise, the quality of your digital painting may suffer.

FIGURE 2.16 Perfect symmetry in a composition makes the viewer uncomfortable, as if something is wrong or unnatural. This image is the most iconic example of the use of symmetrical composition (study done after a screenshot from the movie *The Shining* by Stanley Kubrick (1980).

The effect of symmetry or mirror is to be avoided, except in certain cases, such as to unsettle the viewer or make them understand that something supernatural is happening. Indeed, perfectly symmetrical things are not found in nature, and when your brain perceives something that is, it is unsettled and consequently feels uncomfortable.

The second thing is, as seen earlier, the four main lines you must deal with in composition are the four edges of your painting. You must avoid drawing attention to these to allow for greater immersion.

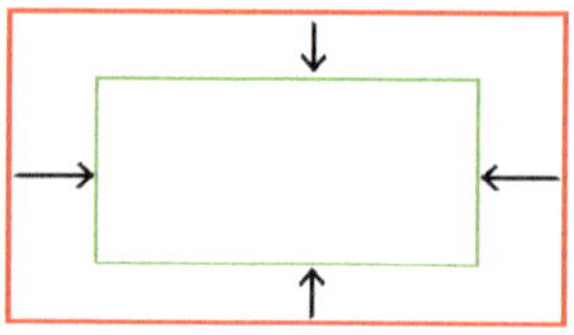

FIGURE 2.17 Avoid drawing too much attention to the borders of the frame to achieve better immersion in your painting.

Hence, the importance of having strong lines that guide the eye toward the points of interest you have chosen (see the 'strong lines' section). You should try to lead the viewer's gaze into your painting, immerse them in the world you are describing to them, and you want them to stay there as long as possible. If you find yourself with focus points or strong contrasts near the edges, the viewer might have difficulty forgetting that they are looking at an image and might not be able to truly immerse himself in your world.

FIGURE 2.18 A good example of an immersive painting. Avoiding strong contrasts near the edges allows the viewers to immerse themselves in the world you are showing them (digital painting done in Photoshop for *Assassin's Creed Valhalla* (*Assassin's Creed* TM & © Ubisoft Entertainment. All Rights Reserved).

STRONG LINES

This is something you might underestimate. Strong lines really enhance the viewer's experience when looking at your image. The viewer appreciates not having to try to understand what is happening, so you must be very clear in your intentions, and leading lines help greatly with this. Take one of your paintings where you find the composition a bit shaky and start making all the strong lines lead, even somewhat crudely, toward your point(s) of interest. You will notice that your painting gains clarity and immediately has a more professional look. It can be quite impressive.

FIGURE 2.19A Example of a digital painting improvable with stronger guiding lines (digital painting created in Photoshop).

FIGURE 2.19B You can use light or modify the direction of strong lines already there to guide the viewer's eye toward the two main points of interest.

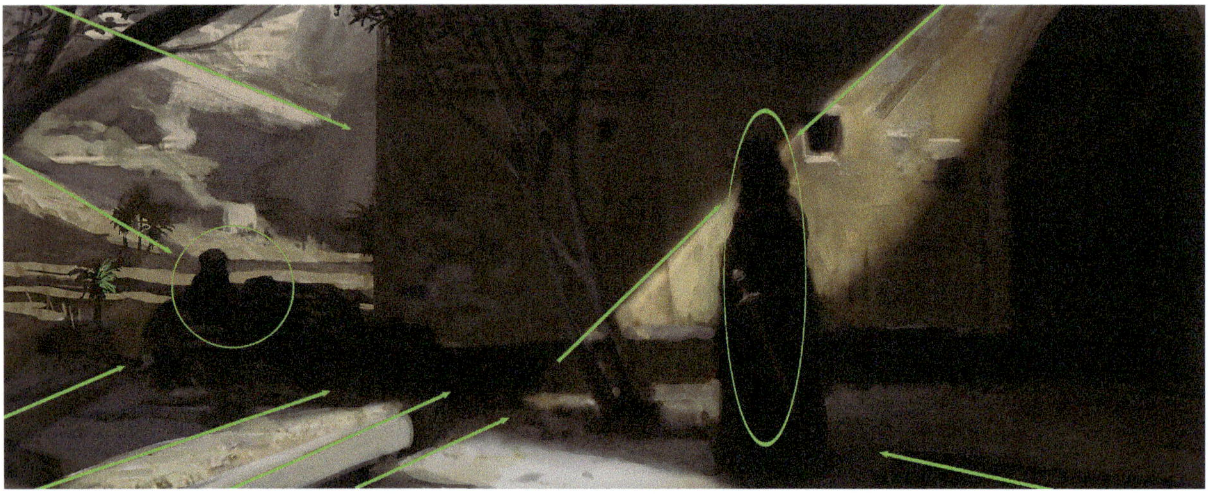

FIGURE 2.19C You can see how these lines guide the viewer's eye more effectively, making it easier to understand what's happening in the image.

PLAY WITH IMAGE PROPORTIONS

Don't hesitate to play a lot with the shapes and proportions in your painting, even if you are already well into the process. Sometimes, you tend to draw things a bit too 'narrowly' and then realize it. If that happens to you, just adjust the proportions by unlocking the aspect ratio in the *image size* settings. This allows you to gain width and give your painting some breathing room.

FIGURE 2.20A Sometimes, your painting might feel a bit 'narrow'. It's time to play with the proportions of your image, especially for this kind of establishing shot, for which you want to convey the feeling of vastness (digital painting done for *Assassin's Creed Valhalla* (*Assassin's Creed* TM & © Ubisoft Entertainment. All Rights Reserved).

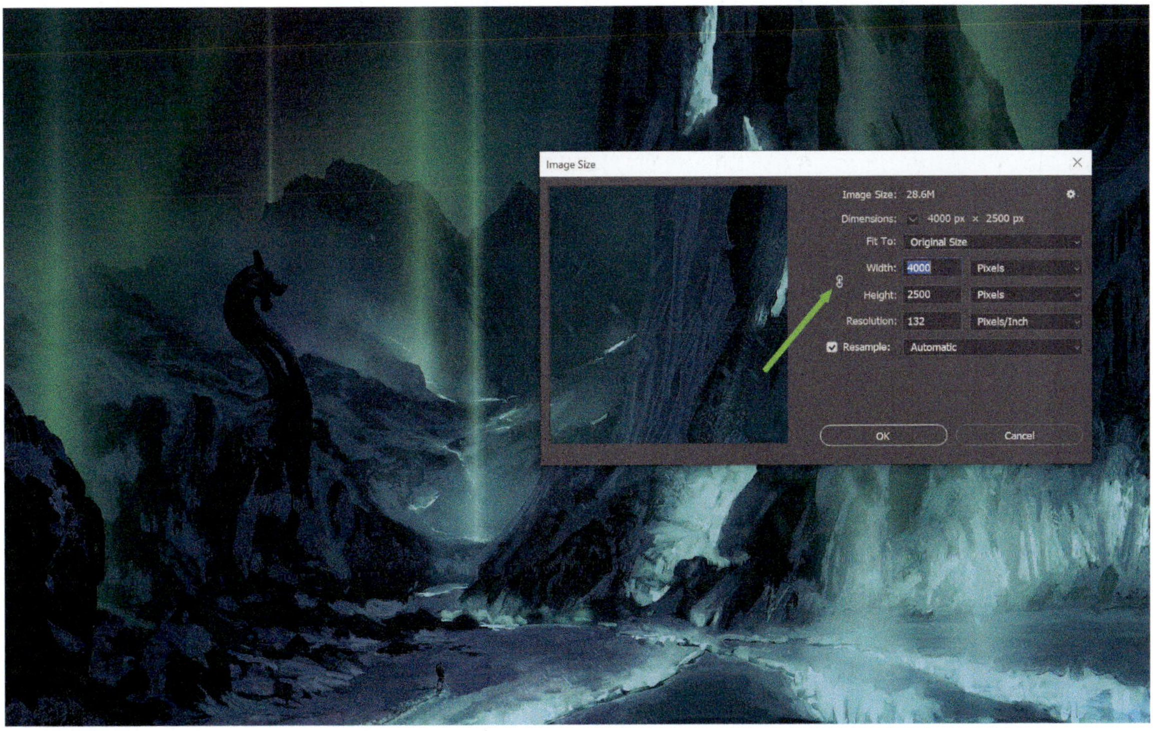

FIGURE 2.20B In this case, you must unlock the proportions of the resizing image menu to be able to deform the image and make it larger.

FIGURE 2.20C In some cases, you must pay attention to some objects or characters that might appear too deformed. You can then adjust them separately.

CROP FOR DRAMA

You might also dramatically crop your image to see if it gives a completely different dimension to the result. It's a good test to do and doesn't commit you to anything; you can always undo it in digital painting, so feel free to experiment.

FIGURE 2.21A Let's see how you can dramatically affect the meaning of this painting by using the crop tool (digital painting done for *Assassin's Creed Unity* (*Assassin's Creed* TM & © Ubisoft Entertainment. All Rights Reserved).

FIGURE 2.21B A dramatic horizontal crop emphasizes the character's movement, adding a sense of speed and urgency, and focuses more on the character's objective.

FIGURE 2.21C On the other hand, a vertical crop will emphasize verticality, highlighting how the environment feels narrow and suffocating. Both versions are valid depending on the message or feeling you want to convey.

SILHOUETTES

As you continuously deal with the fact that you are working with a two-dimensional medium but always want to give your painting maximum depth, and since your goal is to make reading of the image as clear as possible, having well-defined and easily identifiable silhouettes helps a lot. This is why, in many environment concept art pieces, you can often easily distinguish the silhouettes of important landmarks or clearly defined character shapes. This clearly draws the viewer's eye to chosen spots and decisively defines the different plans that will give your painting its depth. These silhouettes are crucial, and it's good to spend time refining them, even if it means being a bit sketchy inside the shape. If the silhouette is well-defined, the viewer will understand what it is and won't rely too much on the details painted inside the silhouette, especially if it's something at a certain distance from the 'camera'.

FIGURE 2.22A Here is an initial sketch where the focus is on the overall shapes and values. It is about placing elements here, but it doesn't look very clean in terms of shape definition.

FIGURE 2.22B You now focus on the important silhouettes, defining them better for improved readability.

FIGURE 2.22C Then, use these silhouettes as selections and paint inside them with shapes that can be very abstract, if they are within the correct range of values and seem logical given the lighting situation.

POSITIVE VERSUS NEGATIVE SHAPES

Shape in painting often refers to what's called a positive shape. For example, the *positive shape* of an orange is a circle. That said, in composition, there is another kind of shape that must be considered, and these are *negative shapes.* These shapes are composed of the spaces between objects or even the openings that you could observe within a *positive shape.* For example, openings in the foliage of a tree. These *negative shapes* do not describe a particular object but rather a space. It is important to consider them with as much attention as when dealing with *positive shapes.* Therefore, it is necessary to avoid repetitions of similar shapes, mirror effects, and other problems that could diminish the quality of your composition, whether they are *positive* or *negative shapes.*

FIGURE 2.23A This is a very good example of well-balanced positive and negative shapes. There is a lot of variety, with no repetition in the shapes (Vincent van Gogh (1853–1890), *Vase with Irises*, oil on canvas, 1890).

FIGURE 2.23B Here are the positive shapes in white (contours of the objects); you can notice a nice variety. Even with only these two values, the design looks interesting.

FIGURE 2.23C Now, focus on the negative shapes (in white). The negative shapes are the spaces between the positive shapes. These need to be well thought out as well. No boring repetitions, no awkward mirroring.

FIGURE 2.23D Now, let's do the exercise of modifying this painting to have a design of positive and negative shapes that is less well thought out. By modifying the angle of the bouquet so that it is parallel to the angle of the table and the frame of the canvas, the painting already looks less visually interesting.

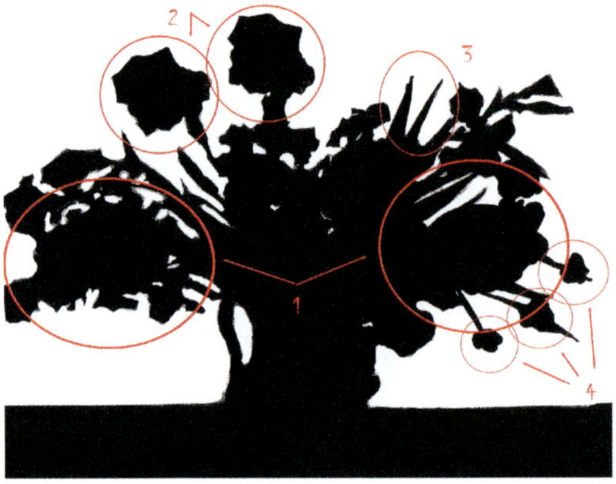

FIGURE 2.23E You can also note the mirroring of the two shapes on either side of the vase (1), the repetition of the flower shape at the top (2), the repetition of the leaf shape (3), and the triple repetition of the flower shape on the right (4), all at the same distance from each other. In short, in just a few minutes, you can completely ruin a beautiful design. It's much easier to do this than to pay close attention to these designs of positive and negative shapes. So be aware of that and focus when you paint any shape in your digital painting.

TANGENTS AND REPETITIONS

Now that your composition seems set, take one last look and see if you can spot two things that can ruin a digital painting: *repetitions* and *tangents*.

When talking about *repetition*, it refers to shapes that repeat, whether they are positive shapes or negative shapes, as seen previously. You must avoid boring the viewer, as this is a perfect example of something that can cause them to lose interest in your image in no time. It's a mistake that you'll make regularly, even after years of practice. Because it turns out that your brain loves things to be well-ordered and well-placed because it's easier to categorize and therefore recognize them. It's a survival reflex. In everyday life, you must be able to quickly recognize the objects around you to navigate the world without constantly bumping into things or, worse, getting hit by a bus. Therefore, the brain is continuously in this 'survival' mode, even when you are painting. So, if you don't pay attention, you will start to 'organize' your shapes logically and orderly. You will paint a series of rocks, for example, or trees, and paint them all the same size and all equidistant from each other. It's almost automatic. However, if you focus before each brushstroke, you will immediately fight against this reflex and try to place your shapes interestingly or find a camera angle that makes these objects, even though they are identical, appear to have different sizes and shapes in relation to one another.

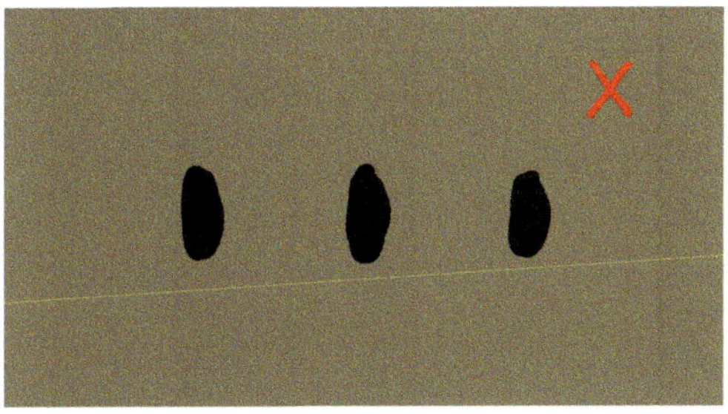

FIGURE 2.24A Here is a simplified example of how your mind will try to organize the shapes in your digital painting. And it will be the same for each of them if you don't pay attention, and this will happen throughout your career! So, you need to step back and try to spot these organizations that make your composition look uninteresting and non-harmonious. You will notice that the shapes are of equal size, equally spaced, and centered. This is really to be avoided. This most often happens when painting bushes, characters, rocks, trees, etc.

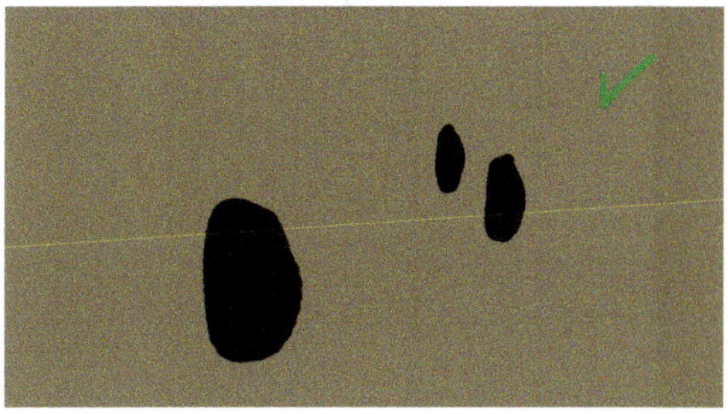

FIGURE 2.24B Here is a better way to paint those same shapes. Sizes and distances are irregular; they don't occupy the same space in the composition. In cases where the objects to paint are of the same size and at the same distance, play with the camera angle and perspective to make them appear different from each other.

The second mistake you might make if you don't pay attention is drawing or painting *tangents*. A *tangent* is a line that joins another line at a single point. These *tangents* can exist in your painting or interact with the edge of the image. You must absolutely avoid this. They are true eye magnets, and nothing can more quickly take the viewer out of your image. The solution is *an overlap*. Instead of having one line join another at a single point, ensure that one line or shape clearly passes over the other, which allows for a clear understanding of which shape is in front of the other. This is an extremely important point. A tangent can completely ruin a composition, while it is very easy to correct.

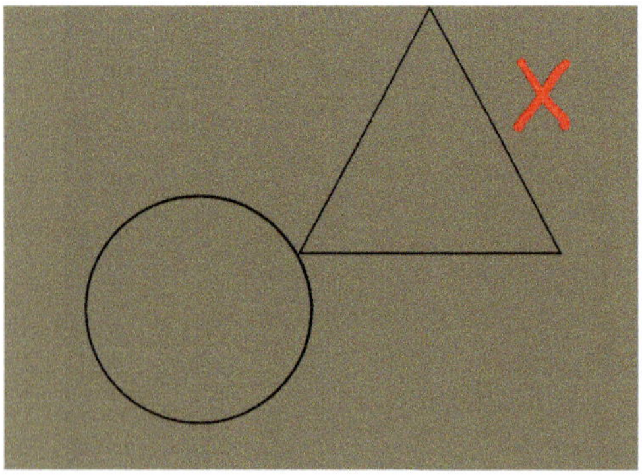

FIGURE 2.25A Here is an example of tangents that attract attention in a bad way. Not only does the triangle have a tangent on the edge of the circle, but also on the frame of the image. This highlights the fact that the frame exists and can draw the viewer's attention away from your painting, and the first tangent makes it difficult to determine which object is in front of the other.

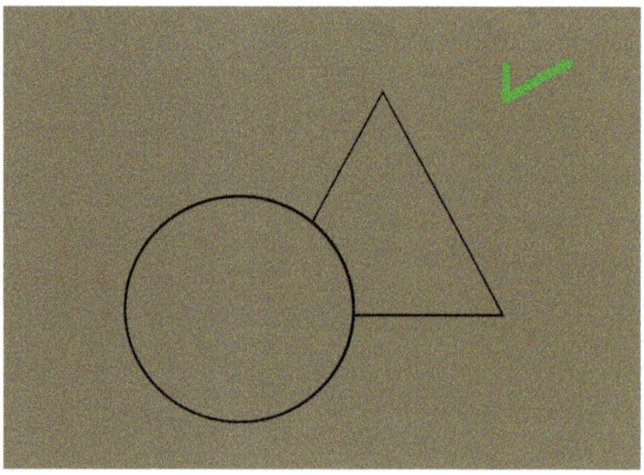

FIGURE 2.25B Here, let's use **clear overlapping** to indicate which object is closest to the viewer. Also, let's reposition the triangle so it's not so close to the edge of the frame. You could even place part of the triangle outside the frame—just make sure its point isn't directed toward the edge. That helps maintain a strong composition and avoids leading the eye out of the image.

It is also important to point out the importance of avoiding a line or shape stopping behind another line or shape. Again, the solution is to overlap. This is very important for giving a sense of depth and making clear where the objects are in space. Indeed, you are dealing with a two-dimensional medium, so it is important to provide as many visual clues as possible to describe where objects are in depth in comparison to one another.

FIGURE 2.25C Here is an example of a digital painting where there are many situations where you must use overlap (digital painting done for *For Honor* (© Ubisoft Entertainment. All Rights Reserved)).

FIGURE 2.25D Notice how the green shapes overlap the red shapes, clearly defining the position of the objects in space. Also note that the character does not have any overlap. As a result, its position in space is a bit difficult to read.

FIGURE 3.1 A good example of how to use light to make your painting look more interesting (Digital painting done for *Assassin's Creed Unity*; *Assassin's Creed* TM & © Ubisoft Entertainment. All Rights Reserved).

CHAPTER 3

Light and Values

DOI: 10.1201/9781003536703-4

TECHNICAL TERMS

Before really talking about light, it is good to recall the definitions of the technical terms:

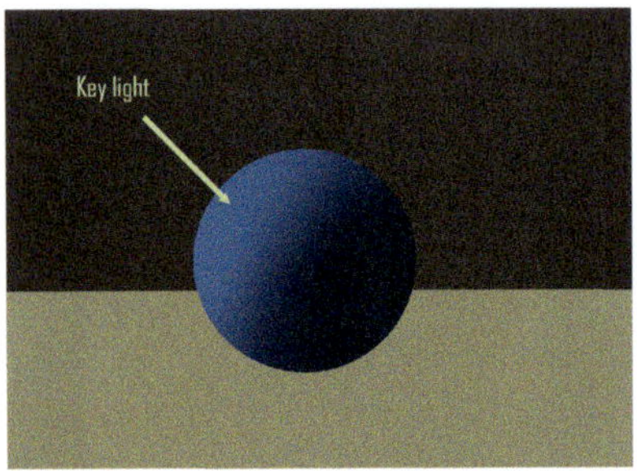

FIGURE 3.2A Here the key light comes from the top left.

Key Light

A key light is the primary light source. It is the main light that defines the form, shape, and texture of the subject. For example, for a daylight exterior environment, the sun is your key light.

FIGURE 3.2B A backlight added.

Backlight

A backlight, also known as rim light, is a light source placed behind the subject, often above and to the side, to create a rim of light around the subject's edges. By illuminating the edges of the subject, it creates a clear distinction and prevents the subject from blending into the background, enhancing the three-dimensionality of the scene.

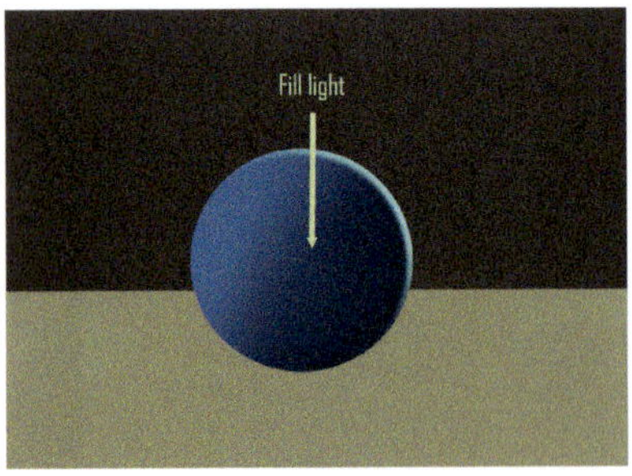

FIGURE 3.2C The fill light opens the shadow.

Fill Light

A fill light is a secondary light source used to reduce the contrast created by the key light. It helps to ensure that details in the shadowed areas are visible and that the overall image is not too high in contrast. For an outdoor environment painting, the fill light could be the sky or a bounce light.

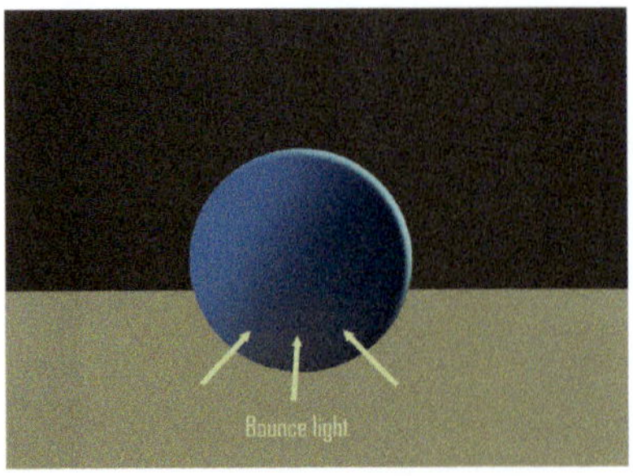

FIGURE 3.2D The bounce light takes on the color of the object it bounces off.

Bounce Light

A bounce light is a more diffused light achieved by directing a light source (such as a key light or fill light) at a reflective surface, which then bounces the light back onto the subject. The main purpose of bouncing light is to soften and spread out the light, reducing harsh shadows and creating more natural, even illumination. Painting a bounce light will really give richness to your painting.

Specular

Referring to the mirror-like reflection of light from a surface, where the light is reflected at a single angle, creating a highlight. Specular reflections are usually characteristic of shiny or glossy surfaces, where the angle of incidence equals the angle of reflection, resulting in bright, concentrated spots of light. Nevertheless, you still find specular on almost all surfaces, but it can be diffuse depending on the type of material.

FIGURE 3.2E First example of a possible type of specular, a diffuse one.

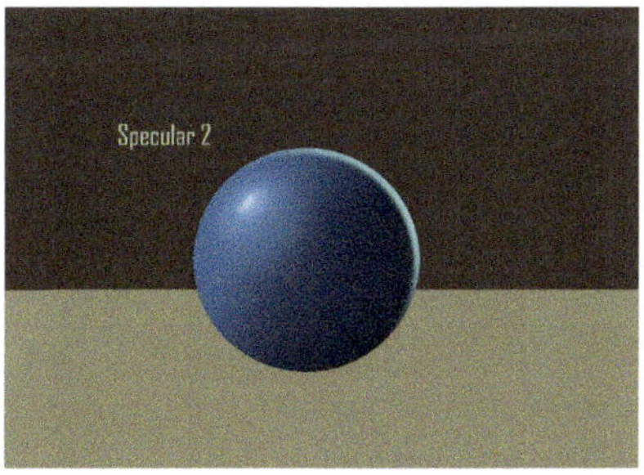

FIGURE 3.2F A sharper specular means the surface is smoother and more reflective.

Mid Tone

A midtone is a color or value located on the illuminated side of the object, right next to the area where the shadow begins. It is often in the mid tones that you find the true local color of an object, as this color is not significantly influenced by the key light and is also not overly affected by the fill light or the shadow colors.

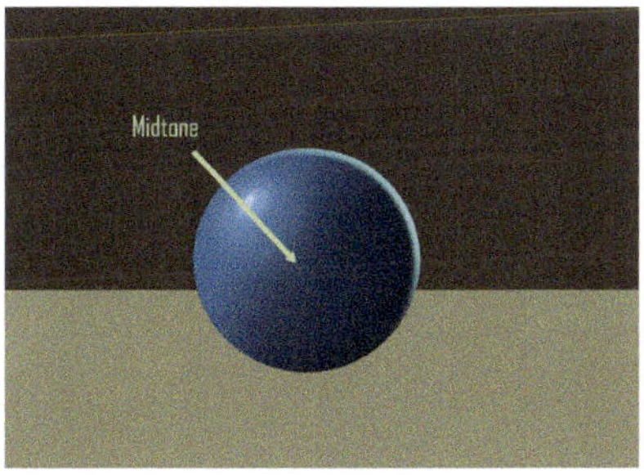

FIGURE 3.2G Midtone.

FIGURE 3.2H Here are some examples of midtones: surfaces that are still in the key light but are turning away from it. The 'true' color of the skin should be here (John Singer Sargent (1856–1925), *Self-Portrait* (1892), oil on canvas).

Shadow

A shadow is the area on an object or surface that receives no direct light from the primary light source. Shadows help define the form and create a sense of depth in a painting. Shadows can vary in intensity and color based on the light sources and the surfaces they fall upon.

FIGURE 3.2I The shadow area is the part of the object that is not lighted by the key light.

Core Shadow

A core shadow refers to the darkest area on an object where little to no direct light reaches. This area is typically found opposite the light source and does not include surfaces touched by bouncing light.

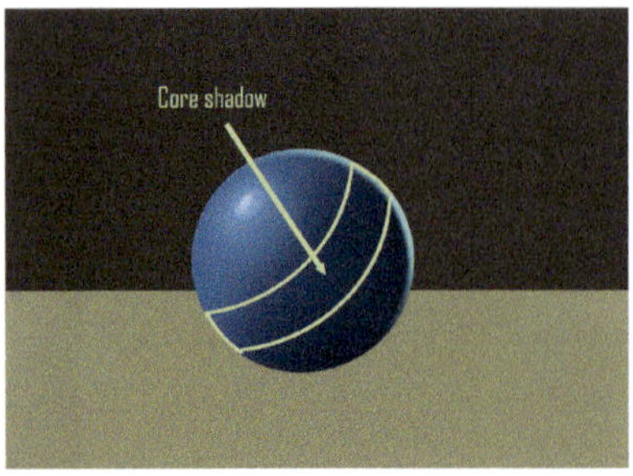

FIGURE 3.2J The area of the core shadow.

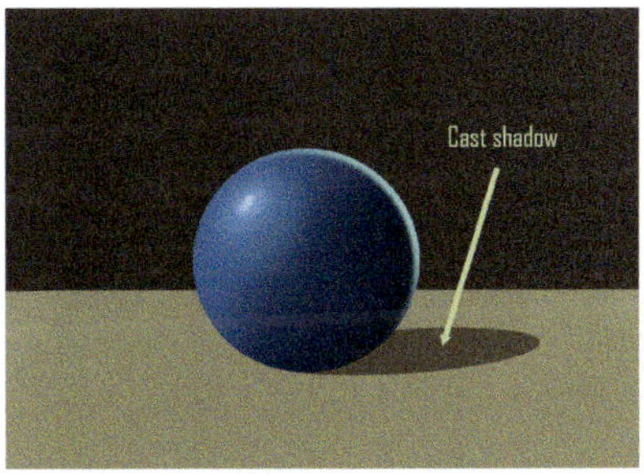

FIGURE 3.2K The cast shadow.

FIGURE 3.2L This cast shadow provides information that the surface it is cast on is flat and smooth.

FIGURE 3.2M This cast shadow provides information that the surface it is cast on is irregular.

FIGURE 3.2N This surface now looks very irregular. Changing the shape of a cast shadow can make a surface appear very different. Keep that in mind when you paint any cast shadow and be aware of the surface it is cast on.

Cast Shadow

A cast shadow is the dark area created on a surface when an object blocks a light source. Unlike contact shadows, which occur where an object touches a surface, cast shadows extend from the object in the direction opposite to the light source. These shadows provide crucial information about the direction and quality of the light and help to define the spatial relationship between objects in a scene, enhancing the overall sense of depth and three-dimensionality. The shape of the cast shadow will also provide a strong clue about the shape of the object casting it.

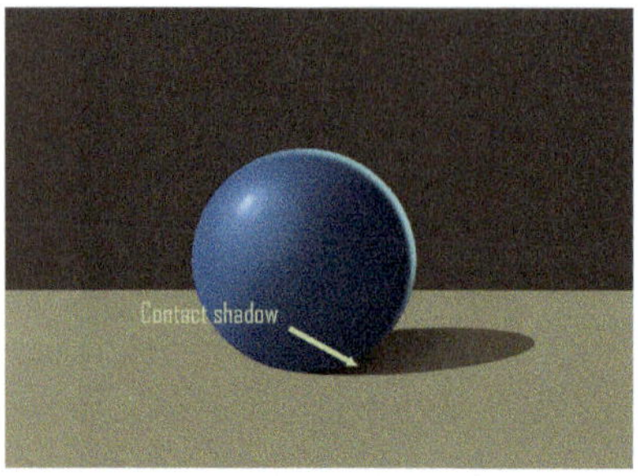

FIGURE 3.2O The contact shadow makes the object appear more grounded on the surface.

FIGURE 3.2P Here is the result that has been started with a dark blue circle and painted logically, considering how this object should react to the light. Keep this mindset every time you paint something.

Contact Shadow/Occlusion

A contact shadow, also known as occlusion, is the dark area where two surfaces meet and light is obstructed from reaching the point of contact. This type of shadow is usually the darkest and most defined shadow in a painting, as it occurs where light is least likely to penetrate. Contact shadows enhance the realism of a painting by grounding objects and creating a sense of solidity and depth.

HOW LIGHT WORKS

You should ask yourself: How do you perceive light? How does your mind use it to recognize the environment around you? No need to go into scientific details here, but let's try to explain in simple terms how light works. By understanding this principle, you'll be able to paint images from your imagination with believable lighting.

Light always comes from a source that needs to be identified. By doing this, you'll be able to define its direction and quality and thus deduce what kind of shadows you need to paint (hard or soft) and in which direction they should fall in. This light falls on your environment and allows the viewer to understand the shape of the things. Your mind can identify a shape by deduction, observing the contrast between forms in the light and those in the shadows. This is why it's crucial to distinguish what is illuminated and what remains in shadow, even when the light source is weak.

First, try to determine the main light source on the object you need to paint. This light source can be the key light, but if you're painting an object that is entirely in the shadow, you need to consider that its primary light source might be something else, like the sky.

FIGURE 3.3 In this example, the sun doesn't really affect what can be seen. In this case, the main light source is the very diffuse light coming from the cloudy sky (digital painting done in Photoshop for *For Honor* (© Ubisoft Entertainment. All Rights Reserved).

If you have a strong key light, there will be bounce light, meaning the light source will bounce off surfaces and become a sort of secondary light that illuminates the objects. Adding these light sources will greatly enhance the realism of your scene.

FIGURE 3.4 On the left side of the painting, note that this entire area is not directly affected by the key light. Here, the main light sources are the sky and the bounce light coming from the right side (digital painting done in Photoshop for *Assassin's Creed Revelations* (*Assassin's Creed* TM & © Ubisoft Entertainment. All Rights Reserved).

In summary, it's recommended to determine the local value of an object first (light or dark). Indeed, a dark object will react differently to light compared to a light object.

FIGURE 3.5A Here is an example of three objects with very different values (dark, mid-tone, and bright) that all react differently to the same light source. It is interesting to study this in detail by attempting to paint this scene. Let's describe step-by-step what should happen in your mind when painting something. You will then be able to understand the logic and apply it later in your digital paintings when you need to paint from your imagination.

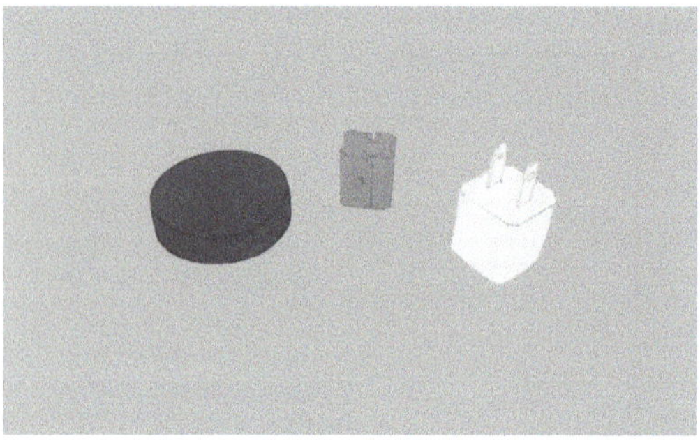

FIGURE 3.5B It is good to start by thinking first about the value and local color of each object. Which one is the darkest, which one is the lightest, and compare them to each other so that the differences are clear.

Then, identify the key light (the main light source in your scene) and paint the objects affected by this light, being aware of its strength and direction.

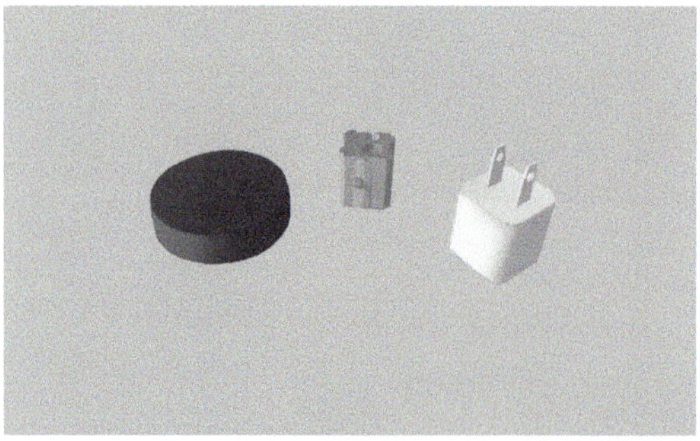

FIGURE 3.5C It is always important to clearly define where the main light source is coming from in your scene. This way, you can paint darker values on the sides of objects that the key light does not reach. Note that the shadow values of very light objects can be brighter than the lit sides of very dark objects.

Paint the cast shadows logically, in the direction opposite to the key light's position, and estimate their length based on the height of the key light. Make sure to be aware of the shape of the object the shadow is cast on.

FIGURE 3.5D Cast shadows must go in the direction opposite to the light source casting them. You need to consider the shape of the object casting the shadow and the shape of the object on which the shadow is cast (in this case, the surface is flat, so the shadow does not take on a particular shape except for the shape of the object casting it).

Finally, identify the secondary lights (fill light and bounce lights).

FIGURE 3.5E Addition of fill light (coming from above and the sides) and bounce light (coming from the table), as well as contact shadows (the areas that light reaches with difficulty, and the occlusion that objects produce on surrounding objects).

Always keep in mind the logic of how light works. Aim to have consistent lighting; otherwise, your painting won't appear solid.

Of course, this doesn't apply to very stylized, 2D cartoon painting, where the logic of light doesn't really apply most of the time. In this case, you'll focus more on local values, local colors and the shape of objects.

DEALING WITH MULTIPLE LIGHT SOURCES

It's one of the challenges of thinking like a lighting designer when painting. If that's the case, you think about key light, fill light, backlight, and stay within that logic. However, in some cases, like a night concept art or an interior scene, you may have to deal with multiple light sources, so several lights might be considered as key lights. You must think in terms of zones. In one zone, a light source will be more influential and considered the main light source, while in another zone, that same light will have no influence. Generally, you also keep some sort of diffuse light (which can be weak) that illuminates the entire scene uniformly (like the influence of moonlight, for example).

FIGURE 3.5F Adding another strong light source on the right side makes the core shadows more visible and the cast shadows less present.

FIGURE 3.6 Times Square in New York City is a great example of a place where the multitude of light sources creates a single diffuse light source. Notice the very soft cast shadows (photography by Claire Jones via Unsplash).

In some cases, multiple light sources can be considered as part of the same overall light source. For example, if you paint a scene set in Times Square, New York, at night, all the lights and neon signs could logically be considered individual light sources. However, if you closely observe photo references, you'll notice they merge into one large light source that casts a single diffuse shadow, which would be somewhat equivalent to the lighting quality of a large diffuse light source like the sky.

Always try to think logically about how light works. It's important to understand its physical behavior and to observe your environment daily, noting how objects react in different lighting situations. Therefore, the importance of researching visual references and attentive daily observation shouldn't be underestimated. This helps build a visual bank that assists in deducing how light acts in various situations. It's one reason why great artists advise doing visual studies. Study what you see around you as often as possible. Not only will this improve your drawing skills (by strengthening your ability to copy observed shapes), but it will also enrich your visual bank and help you better understand how light behaves in different scenarios. You can also practice this mentally when you must wait (at a bus stop, for example). Try to observe your surroundings. Note how the light reacts. Think about which values you would use for one shape compared to another. This will greatly benefit you in the long run.

With experience, you'll realize there's a scientific logic behind it all, and the more you master and understand how light works, the better you'll be at painting any situation from your imagination.

FIGURE 3.7 Painting from your imagination is easier when you understand how light works. Here, the cast shadows are painted logically in relation to the position of the key light. The values all react differently to the same light source, and you can feel the fill light from the sky and the bounce lights coming from the objects directly hit by the light. (Digital painting done in Photoshop for *Assassin's Creed III* (*Assassin's Creed* TM & © Ubisoft Entertainment. All Rights Reserved).

PLAY WITH VALUES

Let's emphasize the huge importance of choosing the right values for digital painting. Having the correct values almost guarantees success. However, this doesn't mean you should use as many values as possible. In fact, the opposite is true. The more you limit the number of values in your painting, the more interesting the result will be.

FIGURE 3.8A Here is a good example of a digital painting in which a very limited range of values was used (digital painting done in Photoshop for *Assassin's Creed Unity* (*Assassin's Creed* TM & © Ubisoft Entertainment. All Rights Reserved).

FIGURE 3.8B If you look at this painting in grayscale, you can better see the narrow value range.

FIGURE 3.8C Let's simplify the shapes and values even more so you can see that only four to five values were used.

Therefore, try to merge values that are close to each other. For example, if you have a character in front of a wall, try to make one or more shapes of the character have the same value as the background. Then, play with the hue or color temperature to distinguish them. But the fact that the values are the same will make the painting more interesting to look at.

FIGURE 3.9A In this example, the values of the wall, the clothing, the blade of the sword, and the character's skin are similar, only the hues vary.

FIGURE 3.9B By removing all color information, the desired effect becomes clear. Here, the shape formed by the hair is highlighted.

FIGURE 3.9C By making other artistic choices, one can achieve a different, yet equally valid result. This time, the value of the hair and the sword's hilt blend into the background.

FIGURE 3.9D This time, the eyes become more important in the composition. Many different versions can work; that's where your artistic tastes come into play. Have fun!

Here's another important aspect to keep in mind: Always consider the abstract value of your painting. If your painting didn't represent anything and was just a collection of shapes and colors, would it still have value? Would it be interesting to look at? You need to ask yourself this question. A good test for this is to apply a filter in Photoshop, such as *dust and scratches*. If the result remains interesting without being recognizable, then your painting has the sought-after abstract quality and will stand out.

FIGURE 3.10A Here is an example of digital painting. Let's study his value design (digital painting done in Photoshop for *For Honor* (© Ubisoft Entertainment. All Rights Reserved).

FIGURE 3.10B If you simplify the values, you can then observe the value design, where you see most dark values with two areas of lighter values of different sizes. Even without clearly distinguishing the subject of the painting, the image remains interesting to look at from an abstract perspective.

VALUE DESIGN

Playing with values also means comparing lighter values with darker ones. Is there a good harmony when comparing them? Is there a connection between all the dark values, or are they scattered chaotically? Is the balance between dark and light values well thought out? One of the two groups should generally dominate the other; it's usually best to avoid them being equal. This is what can be called 'value design', though it is not certain that it's the academic term. Regardless, the important thing is to understand that beyond the subject, colors, and lighting, there is a design of value patterns that is very well thought out in some works.

It's interesting to particularly notice this when you closely study the paintings of the great masters of the 19th century. The subject of the painting becomes an excuse, an opportunity to paint this abstract quality made of light and dark, which makes the painting interesting even from 15 meters away. Back then, artists had to catch the eye of critics and buyers in galleries, and the competition was fierce! You should maintain this way of thinking. Try to make your painting attract the eye in an elegant and intriguing way, regardless of the subject. Value design is one of the fundamental keys to achieving this.

FIGURE 3.11A A composition such as this one is not improvised. The values of each element are carefully chosen (*Madame X*, oil on canvas, John Singer Sargent (1856–1925)).

FIGURE 3.11B The artist's intention was clearly to highlight the whiteness of the subject's skin, which contrasts with the darkness of the rest of the décor. Also, the position of the subject ensures that this lighter form is not completely symmetrical.

FIGURE 3.12A Another interesting composition where the choice of values and their position in the frame is notable (*Staircase in Capri*, 1878, oil on canvas, John Singer Sargent (1856–1925)).

FIGURE 3.12B By greatly simplifying the forms, one can understand the underlying design that makes this painting so interesting to look at.

FIGURE 3.13A Another interesting design where the artist clearly considered the highly contrasting values of the piano to choose the values of the dress and the floor. It is important to know that a portraitist like Sargent would select the dresses that women would wear during sittings with these value relationships in mind. I'm not sure that the floor and the vase were of this color and value on set. Everything here is carefully designed (*Madame Ramon Subercaseaux*, oil on canvas, John Singer Sargent).

FIGURE 3.13B This is the kind of simplification you should make in your mind to understand the value design behind each painting.

KEYS

There are different 'keys' in art, found both in music and painting. In painting, it refers to the range of values that will be used during the creation of the artwork. You might use them unconsciously without knowing their names, but it's always better to be aware of them to use them effectively.

Most of the time, the full range of available values is simplified into 9 or 10 distinct values.

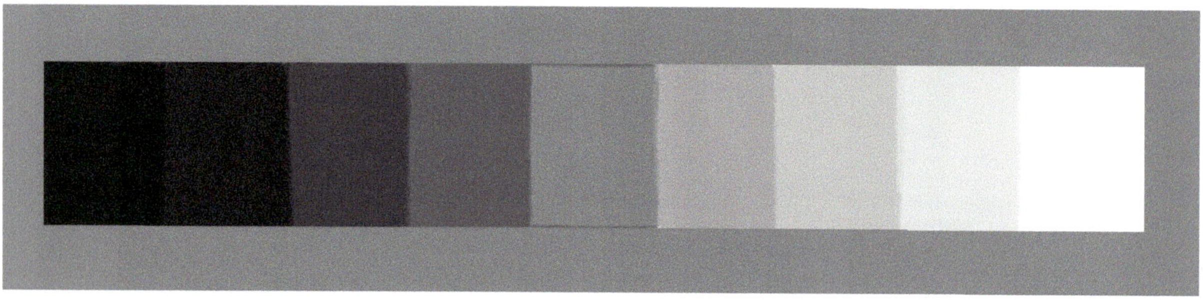

FIGURE 3.14A The value scale with nine different values, from black to white.

FIGURE 3.14B An extended key painting uses the entire value range, from pure white to black, resulting in a very contrasted outcome (*Crucifixion of Saint Peter* (1601), oil on canvas by Caravaggio (1571–1610)).

You can choose to work with all the available values. In this case, it's called an *extended key*. This will result in very high contrast between the lightest and darkest values, like in a Caravaggio painting.

If you choose to work with only a very limited range on the value scale, it's called a *narrow key*. This will have minimal contrast within the lights, mid-tones, or darks. Think of certain Monet paintings, for example.

FIGURE 3.15A This narrow key painting uses little difference between the lightest light and the darkest dark (*Charing Cross Bridge*, 1899, oil on canvas by Claude Monet (1840–1926).

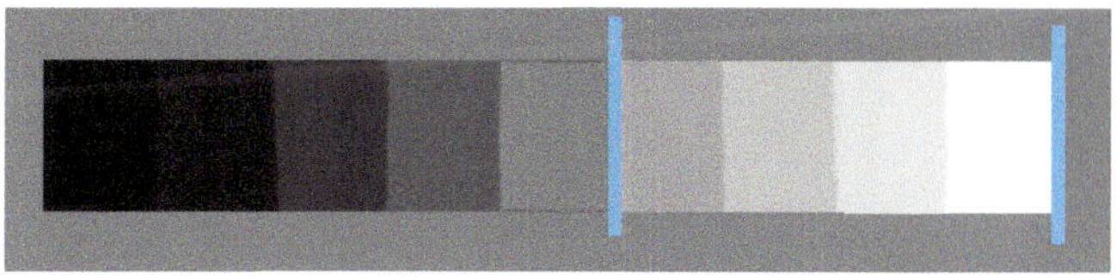

FIGURE 3.15B Here is the value range used here.

A *high key* painting will predominantly use light values, but without completely avoiding dark values; however, darks should remain very minimal, like in this painting by Sargent.

FIGURE 3.16A High key paintings like this one give a sense of intense light (*two boys on a beach with boats* (1878), oil on canvas by John Singer Sargent (1856–1925)).

FIGURE 3.16B Most of the surface is painted with high values, with a few areas containing very dark ones, which makes the scene appear exceptionally bright by contrast.

As you might guess, if you predominantly use dark values, you'll have a *low-key* painting, and if you mostly use middle values, you'll have a *middle key* painting.

FIGURE 3.17A Middle key painting (*Impression, Sunrise*, 1872, oil on canvas by Claude Monet (1840–1926).

FIGURE 3.17B Low key painting (*A Backwater at Wargrave*, 1887, oil on canvas, John Singer Sargent (1856–1925).

You can, of course, make combinations such as a *high key* and *narrow key* painting. In this case, you'll exclusively use values in the very light range. Mastering these principles will allow you to control the mood of your painting and, therefore, convey certain emotions through it.

MID VALUES FIRST, THEN EXTREMES

When starting out in painting, there's a tendency to work with too many value contrasts, making the painting difficult to look at. The viewer doesn't know where to focus their attention and quickly moves on to another image. This is often due to painting a shape that is too bright or too dark early in the process, making it hard to coordinate subsequent values, resulting in an image that is extremely difficult to read.

Here is a suggestion for an exercise you can do, which can easily become a working habit: Start with only mid-values. This means painting only with light mid-values and dark mid-values. So, you stay between 3 and 7, or even 4 and 6 on a value scale, and try to progress as far as possible using only this range.

The result can be surprising. You'll realize that you can go quite far with just these few values without needing the others. However, towards the end of the painting process, have fun adding a strong value contrast at a chosen spot (the focal point of your image, most of the time). You can then use values 1–2 and 8–9. You'll find that your digital painting becomes easy to read, clear, and pleasant to look at. The viewer will enjoy lingering on it, which is obviously the goal. Try playing with this notion, and you'll likely be surprised by the results. Be aware that John Singer Sargent used this technique most of the time, allowing him to maintain complete control over the values until the final stages.

FIGURE 3.18A A rapid sketch with only mid-dark values to show you that it's possible to have something interesting without necessarily needing to go to the extreme values.

FIGURE 3.18B By choosing the appropriate place to put your most extreme values, you can achieve interesting results. The effect has been exaggerated here, just to show you that the effect can be quite powerful.

ATMOSPHERIC PERSPECTIVE

When creating a digital painting, you must deal with an inevitable parameter that has been a challenge for visual artists for centuries: The fact that your painting remains a two-dimensional medium. Therefore, you must find ways to deceive and give the viewer the impression, even if only for a few moments, that the image they are looking at has depth.

There are several tools to help achieve this, such as overlapping or clearly showing that one object is in front of another object (see the chapter on composition). But another essential technique is called *atmospheric perspective.*

FIGURE 3.19A A concept art with a lot of atmospheric perspective (digital painting done in Photoshop for *Assassin's Creed Unity* (*Assassin's Creed* TM & © Ubisoft Entertainment. All Rights Reserved).

If you've had the chance to attend a film shoot, you notice that before the shots, someone walks around with a smoke generator. This is exactly for the same reason: to create that famous atmospheric perspective, which means having less contrast between the values (darks versus lights) that describe shapes that are far away. The farther away, the less contrast there is. In illustration, don't hesitate to exaggerate this fact, even using an atmospheric perspective on objects that aren't that far away. This trick allows clean silhouettes and makes the image easier to read, while also adding an interesting mood. So don't hesitate to use it, and too much is better than too little in this case.

FIGURE 3.19B Here, a lot of smoke has been used to achieve this atmospheric perspective effect. Note the difference in contrast between darks and lights in the foreground versus the contrast between lights and darks in the background. This doesn't mean everything in the background must be lighter; it means there should be less contrast between lights and darks in the distance (digital painting done in Photoshop over a 3D render for *Assassin's Creed Unity* (*Assassin's Creed* TM & © Ubisoft Entertainment. All Rights Reserved).

FIGURE 4.1 Digital painting done in Photoshop for *Assassin's Creed Origins* (*Assassin's Creed* TM & © Ubisoft Entertainment. All Rights Reserved).

CHAPTER 4

Colors

DOI: 10.1201/9781003536703-5

FIGURE 4.2 The color wheel.

VOCABULARY

Color Wheel

A *color wheel* is a circular diagram that represents the relationships between colors. It arranges colors in a spectrum around a circle, typically showing *primary colors* (P), *secondary colors* (S), and *tertiary colors* (T). The *color wheel* is a fundamental tool in painting and design that helps artists understand and utilize color relationships, harmonies, and contrasts.

Hue

Hue refers to the pure spectrum colors commonly recognized as the names of colors (red, blue, yellow, etc.). It is one of the main properties of a color, defining its position within the spectrum of visible light. In painting, *hue* is used to describe the dominant color family that a particular color belongs to, such as a shade of red, blue, or green, without regard to its intensity (saturation) or lightness (value).

FIGURE 4.3 Regardless of their values or saturations, those colors all share the same hue: green.

Saturation

Saturation refers to the intensity or purity of a color. It measures the degree of how vivid or muted a color appears. High saturation means the color is rich and vibrant, while low saturation results in a color that appears more washed out or dull. In digital painting, adjusting *saturation* can significantly affect the mood and visual impact of the artwork.

FIGURE 4.4 The same hue (blue) but ranging from very saturated to almost grey. Note how the last color seems warmer. In fact, any color next to a cool blue looks warmer.

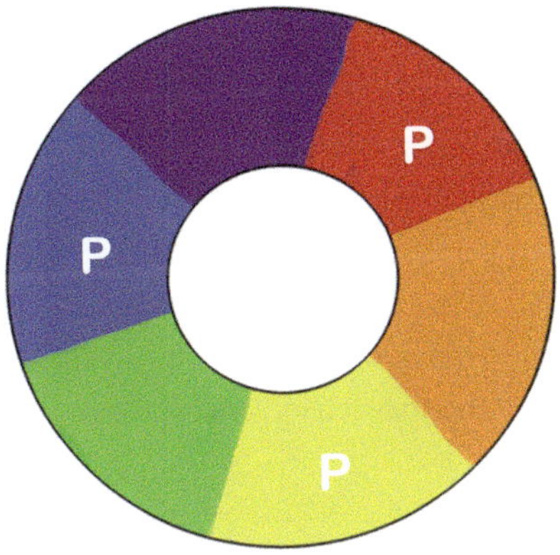

FIGURE 4.5 The Primary colors (P).

Primary Colors

Primary colors are the fundamental colors that cannot be created by mixing other colors together. In traditional color theory, the *primary colors* are red, blue, and yellow. These colors are the building blocks for all other colors in the color wheel and can be combined in various ways to produce a wide range of *secondary* and *tertiary colors.*

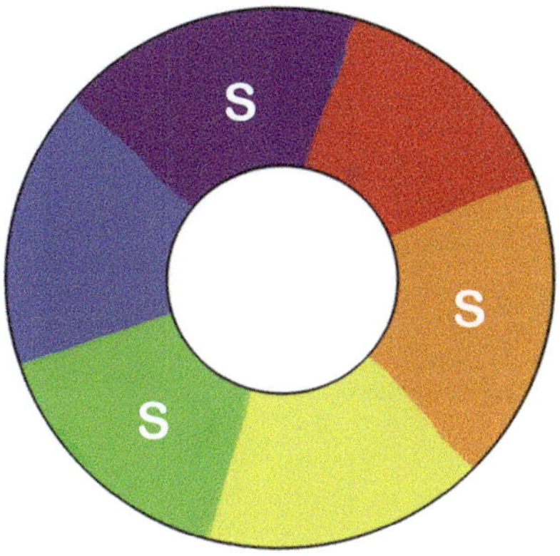

FIGURE 4.6 The secondary colors (S), created by mixing two primary colors together.

Secondary Colors

Secondary colors are colors formed by mixing equal parts of two *primary colors.* In traditional color theory, the *secondary colors* are green, orange, and purple. Specifically, green is created by mixing blue and yellow, orange is created by mixing red and yellow, and purple is created by mixing blue and red. These colors are positioned between the *primary colors* on the *color wheel.*

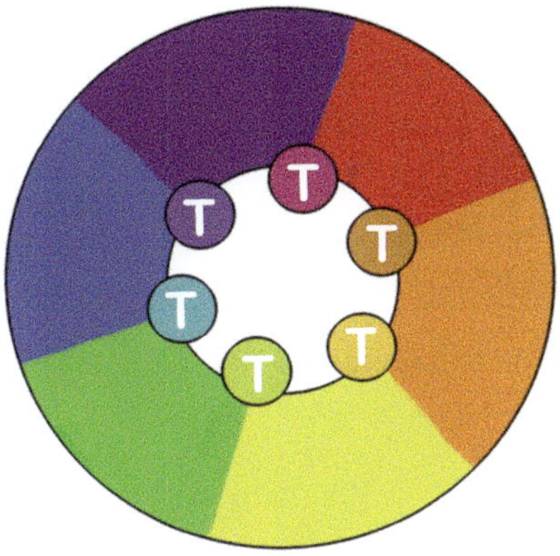

FIGURE 4.7 The tertiary colors (T), created by mixing secondary and primary colors together.

Tertiary Colors

Tertiary colors are colors formed by mixing a *primary color* with a *secondary color* adjacent to it on the *color wheel.* This results in six *tertiary colors*: red-orange, yellow-orange, yellow-green, blue-green, blue-purple, and red-purple. These colors fill the spaces between the *primary* and *secondary colors* on the *color wheel,* creating a more nuanced spectrum of *hues.*

COLOR VERSUS VALUE

The important thing to remember is that mastering values and drawing is far more crucial than mastering colors. That's why I'm only addressing this topic now. If the values you have chosen hold up, then you can use any color, and your digital painting will be readable and interesting. You can't completely ruin a painting with a poor color choice. This is why beginners often struggle with certain images—they focus too much on the colors and don't understand why they can't find the right color to make everything work. In fact, changing the color in such cases won't make a difference. Drawing, composition, and values will always be more important than color choice.

FIGURE 4.8A Here is a version of this digital painting with hue and value information. Now, let's see which of these two pieces of information is more important (Digital painting done in Photoshop for *For Honor* (© Ubisoft Entertainment. All Rights Reserved).

FIGURE 4.8B The same painting without the color information. You can notice that the subject is still readable.

FIGURE 4.8C The same painting with all the color information but with only one value. You can't read anything. It shows how much more important the values are.

However, this doesn't mean that mastering color isn't important. There are some concepts to understand to experiment effectively and ensure that your digital painting is recognized for having a beautiful color harmony, which will certainly enhance the quality of an image that is already solid in other aspects. But don't focus on this too early. If your image seems off, it's certainly not because of your color choices. Keep this in mind.

COLOR HARMONIES

Having a beautiful *color harmony* can indeed make your digital painting stand out. For this, it's good to know what is taught on this subject in Art schools. Should you use these theories daily? May be not. But it is good to know these principles, and to play with them, consciously or not.

In painting theory, *color harmony* refers to the pleasing arrangement and combination of colors. There are several principles and types of *color harmonies* that you can use to create visually appealing and balanced compositions. Here are some of the main types of *color harmonies*:

Analogous Color Harmony

This harmony involves colors that are next to each other on the *color wheel*. They usually match well and create serene and comfortable designs. For example, blue, blue-green, and green.

FIGURE 4.9A Claude Monet often used analogous colors to create harmonious and serene compositions. His use of blues, greens, and purples in these paintings is a great example of this color scheme.

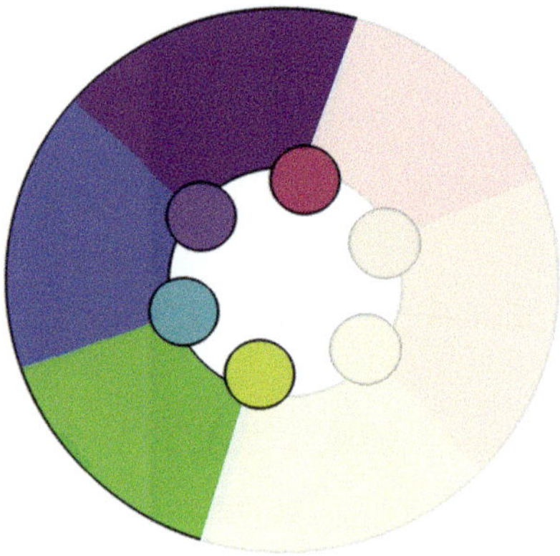

FIGURE 4.9B Here is this analogous color harmony seen on the color wheel.

Complementary Color Harmony

This harmony uses colors that are opposite each other on the *color wheel.* The high contrast between the colors creates a vibrant look, especially when used at full saturation. Examples include red and green, or blue and orange.

FIGURE 4.10A Vincent van Gogh's *Starry Night*—van Gogh used complementary colors like blue and orange to create a vibrant and dynamic composition.

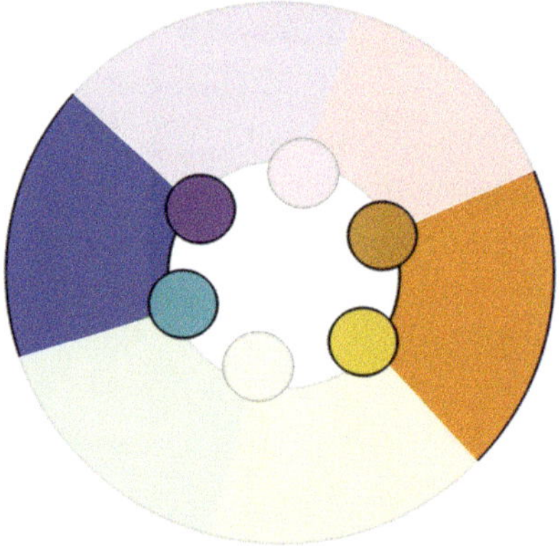

FIGURE 4.10B Example of Complementary color harmony.

Split-Complementary Color Harmony

This is a variation of the complementary *color harmony.* In addition to the base color, it uses the two colors adjacent to its complement. This provides high contrast like the complementary color scheme, but with less tension. For example, if the base color is blue, the split complements would be yellow-orange and red-orange.

FIGURE 4.11A Vincent van Gogh's *The Night Café*—van Gogh used a split-complementary color scheme with red, yellow-green, and blue-green to create a striking and intense atmosphere in this painting.

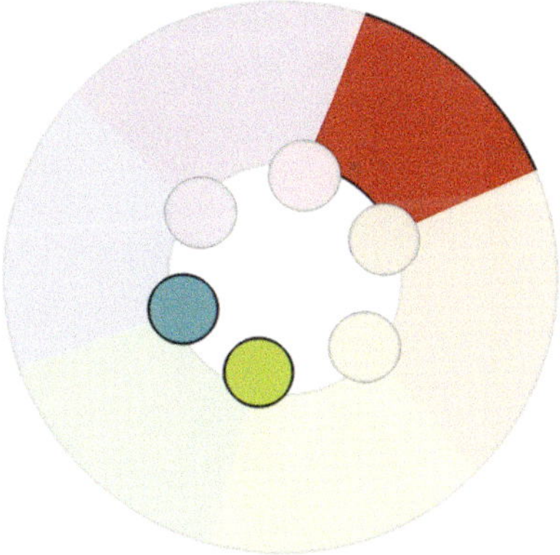

FIGURE 4.11B Example of split-Complementary color harmony.

Triadic Color Harmony

This harmony uses three colors that are evenly spaced around the color wheel. Triadic harmonies are often vibrant, even if the colors are not highly saturated. An example would be red, yellow, and blue.

FIGURE 4.12A Cézanne employed a triadic color harmony using red, blue, and yellow to bring out the richness and depth of the still life.

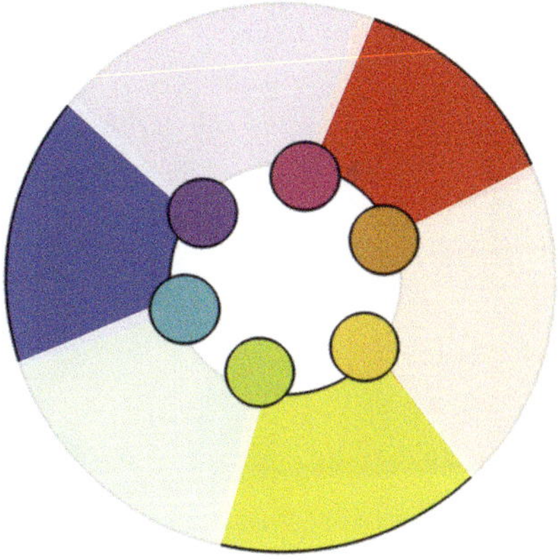

FIGURE 4.12B Example of Triadic color harmony.

Tetradic (Double-Complementary) Color Harmony

This harmony uses two pairs of complementary colors. This is the richest of all the color harmonies because it offers plenty of possibilities for color variation. An example is red and green combined with blue and orange.

FIGURE 4.13A Vincent van Gogh's *Bedroom in Arles*—van Gogh used a tetradic color scheme with blue, orange, red, and green.

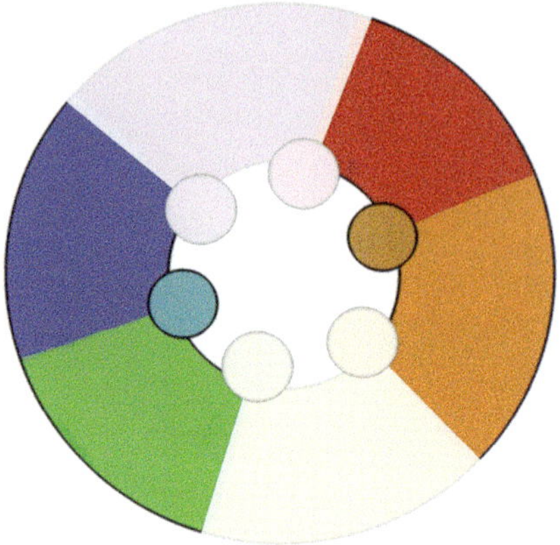

FIGURE 4.13B Example of Tetradic color harmony.

Monochromatic Color Harmony

This harmony involves variations in lightness and saturation of a single color. It uses only one hue with its tints (adding white), shades (adding black), and tones (adding gray). This can create a very cohesive and subtle palette.

FIGURE 4.14A Paul Cézanne's *Mont Sainte-Victoire*—Cézanne employed different tones of green to capture the landscape's essence, giving it a cohesive and serene feel.

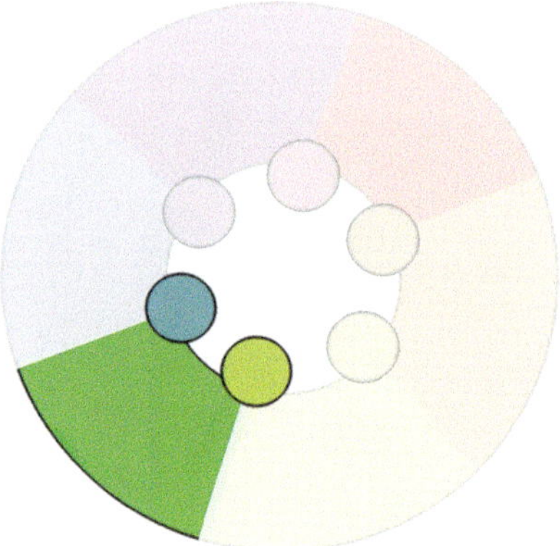

FIGURE 4.14B Example of Monochromatic color harmony.

Achromatic Color Harmony

This harmony uses colors without hue—essentially shades of gray, black, and white. It can be very effective in creating sophisticated and modern looks.

COLOR TEMPERATURE

Colors indeed have a temperature. It's always about defining the temperature of one color relative to another. Thus, when we're on the blue side of the spectrum, we're dealing with the coolest colors, and conversely, when we're on the red/orange side, we're dealing with the warmest colors. However, one blue can be warmer than another blue if it leans toward the blue/green side. The difference can be subtle.

FIGURE 4.15 Cool blues toward the left, warm blues toward the right.

As we've seen, it's very effective to simplify the values in your painting as much as possible and limit them as much as you can. Therefore, when you need to describe a shape but can't really change the value, the option is to play with color temperatures. Varying these temperatures can be very pleasing to the eye; an artist like Claude Monet used this technique a lot, making his paintings appear very lively. Don't hesitate to constantly ask yourself where you could play with these temperature variations.

FIGURE 4.16 Notice how little variation in values there is in the background, only color temperature and hue variations (*The Willows*, oil on canvas, 1885, Claude Monet (1840–1926).

When starting out in painting, you tend to use colors that you find 'dull'. Often, this is because the color temperature isn't suited to the situation. One of the most important things to remember about color temperature is to differentiate the temperatures between what is in the light and what is in the shadow. This is one of the most important things you can learn from Richard Schmid. He said: '*If your key light is a warm light source (like the sun or a candle), the colors in the light will be warmer than those in the shadow. If the key light is a cool light source (like a blue sky), everything in the light will appear cooler than what is in the shadow*'. If you follow this advice, your paintings will never appear dull again; there will be logic that the viewer will accept. They will then find the colors beautiful and harmonious.

It's not about painting everything in the shadow blue and everything illuminated by the sun orange. No, it's subtler than that. In fact, a red object illuminated by the sun will have a warmer red on its lit side and a cooler red on its shadowed side.

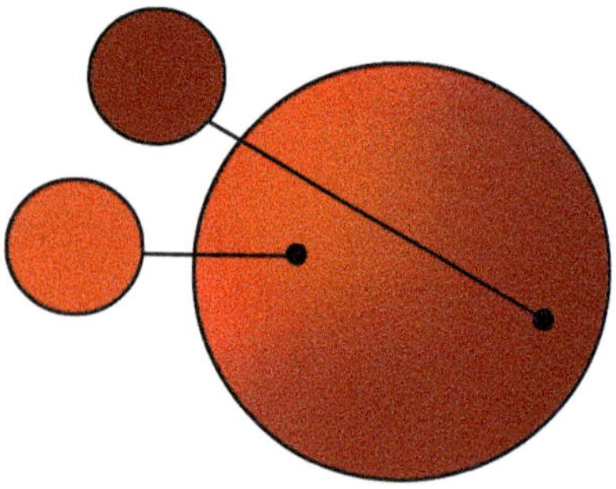

FIGURE 4.17 On the shadow side of this red sphere, the color is darker and cooler compared to the one on the light side, but it's not blue; it's still in the red hues.

Of course, like all rules in art, you can play with this rule and even ignore it and still achieve good results, but knowing this principle can really help you avoid results that appear brown or dull.

COLORS AND EMOTIONS

It often happens that when someone looks at a painting they like, they first talk about the colors. There is indeed a connection between the emotions you can feel when looking at a painting and the colors that were used. This is also true in everyday life. You may react differently to the same landscape depending on the lighting, the colors of the objects, and the mood, which will bring out very different color harmonies. Consequently, you can almost automatically associate certain colors with certain emotions. For example, blue is often associated with calmness and tranquility, but also sadness and melancholy, whereas orange tends to evoke joy, enthusiasm, and warmth. Green is linked to harmony, stability, and nature, while red is often associated with strong emotions like passion, anger, or love.

What can be interesting is to play around with this and experiment with, for example, what an action scene would look like in shades of blue or a calm scene in shades of red. The results can be very intriguing.

FIGURE 4.18 An example of an action scene painted using a cool/neutral color palette (digital painting done in Photoshop for *Assassin's Creed Unity* (*Assassin's Creed* TM & © Ubisoft Entertainment. All Rights Reserved).

FIGURE 4.19 An example of a very calm scene painted using a very warm color palette (digital painting done in Photoshop for *Assassin's Creed Revelations* (*Assassin's Creed* TM & © Ubisoft Entertainment. All Rights Reserved).

FIGURE 5.1 Artwork done in Photoshop for *For Honor* (© Ubisoft Entertainment. All Rights Reserved).

CHAPTER 5

The Process

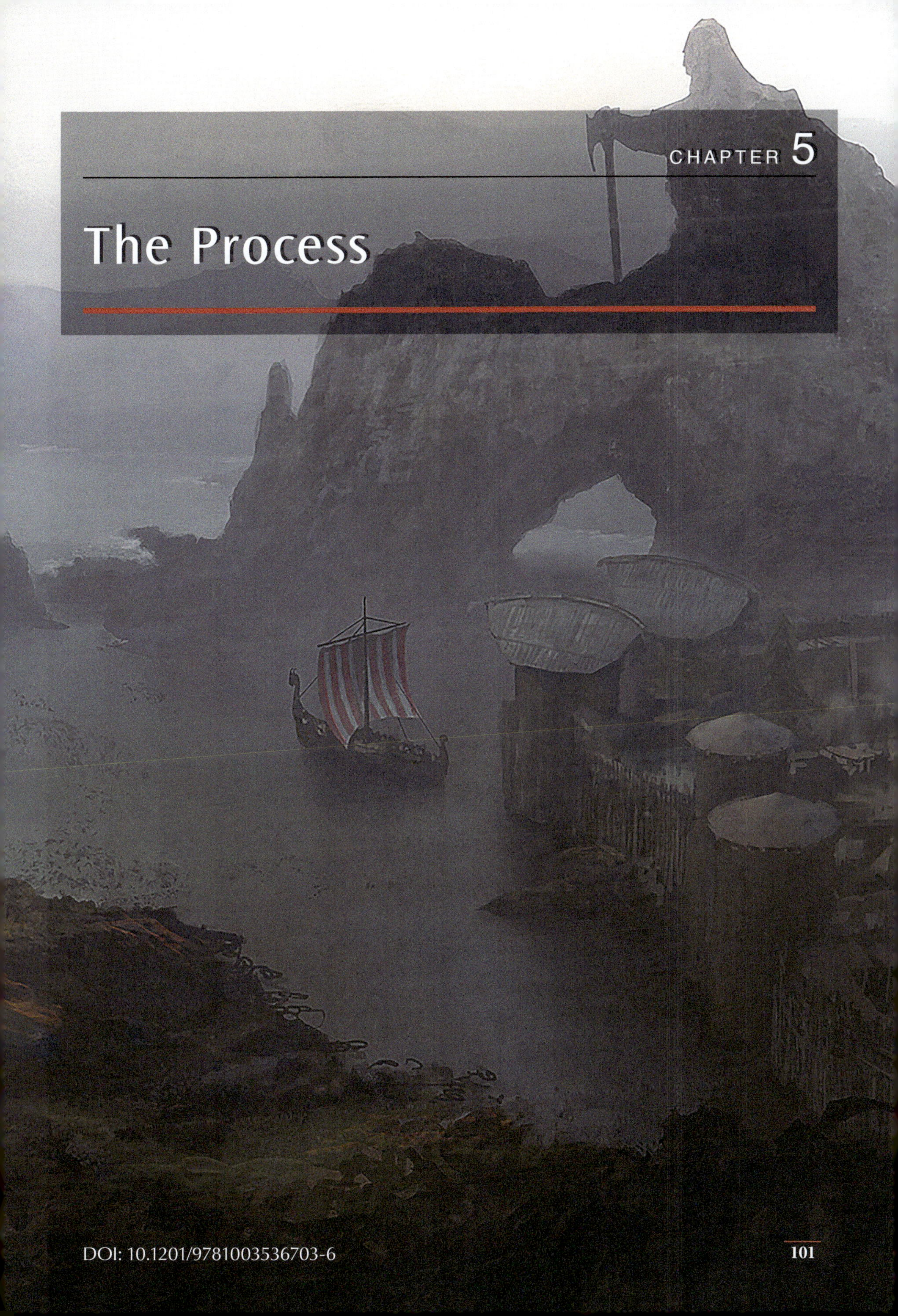

DOI: 10.1201/9781003536703-6

When it comes to digital painting, there isn't a single method. You often must adapt to the time available to complete it, the purpose (whether it's for a mood board, marketing presentation, book cover, storyboard, etc.), and the subject (whether it's a sandstorm in a desert with a single character or a highly detailed painting of a battle between 500 horsemen). Time and methods can really vary depending on these different factors. It's good to test several methods to see the advantages and disadvantages of each, but it's also good to have a reliable method that will succeed every time. When it happens, you don't have much time to experiment. These methods and techniques will be rediscovered and tested throughout your career, and that's where experience counts. The more experience you have, the better you'll be able to adapt your technique to achieve the desired result. However, let's try to describe the kind of method that can be used. The best thing is that you test as many others as possible and thus realize for yourself what works best for you in each situation.

FIGURE 5.2A An example of a painting possible to do in a few hours features a low camera angle, so the viewer can't see many things. There is no complicated architecture close to the 'camera', and no characters are present. The scene is very organic, and many of the elements are in deep shadow. The style is sketchy, so no details are needed (digital painting done in Photoshop for *For Honor* (© Ubisoft Entertainment. All Rights Reserved).

FIGURE 5.2B For this one, you would probably need a few days. The viewer can see the scene from a high angle, so you must paint many elements. It's very detailed, with a lot of different architectural components (digital painting done in Photoshop for *For Honor* (© Ubisoft Entertainment. All Rights Reserved).

THE WAY OF THINKING BEHIND THE TECHNIQUE

Behind the different techniques and approaches described in this book, it's important to understand that the same way of thinking is always at play: using differences in color or value to define shapes. Whether starting with a drawing, a shape, or a 3D base, the thought process remains the same. As already described in Chapter 3, *Light and Values*, you now know how to handle objects of different values under the same lighting. Now, another parameter must be considered: color.

Here, let's use an example with simple shapes, as it makes the explanation easier, but keep in mind that the same method applies to an image with more complex, varied, and numerous shapes.

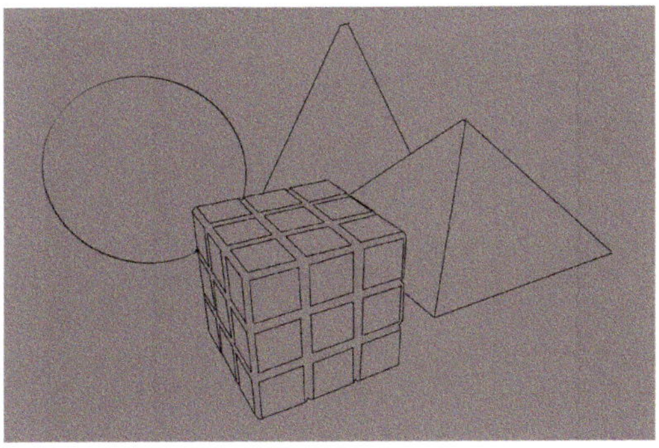

FIGURE 5.3A The first step often involves drawing, which typically begins with a sketch, shapes, or a 3D base. Having a solid drawing as a foundation is the safest way to start a good digital painting.

FIGURE 5.3B Then, determine the value (how light or dark) and the color (hue) of each shape. Some objects, such as this Rubik's Cube, will have multiple values and colors.

FIGURE 5.3C Next, you need to identify the sources of light and where the shadows and cast shadows will be (refer to the chapter on light), as well as how this affects the values and colors.

FIGURE 5.3D When painting, you need to keep in mind something akin to this grid overlaying the shapes. Each of these squares represents a spot that will react differently to light depending on its angle relative to the light sources.

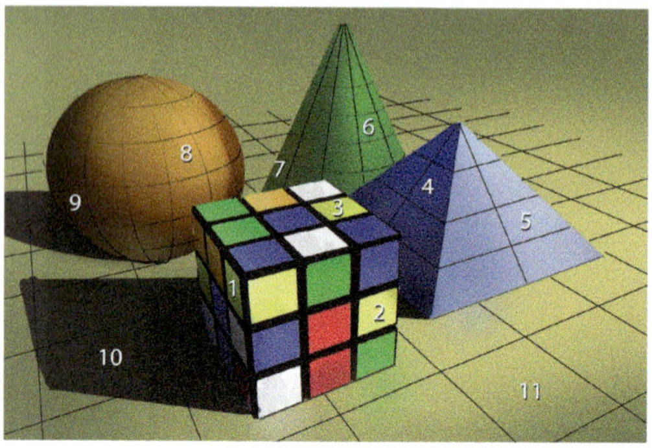

FIGURE 5.3E For square 1, the yellow is darker and cooler because it is in the shadow (in this example, the main light source is warm, and there is a blue sky). For square 2, this light yellow is directly illuminated by the key light, so it appears very bright. For square 3, the same yellow is under nearly identical conditions as square 2, so it looks very similar, with a slight variation in value or color temperature, simply because the angle is a bit different. In square 4, it is a blue that is darker and cooler because its main light source is the blue sky, and it is in shadow relative to the key light. In square 5, the same blue is much brighter and warmer because it is directly facing the sun. The same applies to square 6, which also faces the sun, but its base color is darker, while maintaining its identity (it clearly remains a green). In square 7, the same color is in shadow, making it darker and cooler, but it is slightly warmed by the light bouncing off the orange sphere. In square 8, an orange in full light results in a very bright and warm color. In square 9, this orange is much darker because it is in shadow, with a bit of bounce light from the lit ground. In square 10, a dark brown appears in shadow but is slightly lit and cooled by the sky. In square 11, a bright and warm yellow ochre is illuminated by the key light.

You must approach painting this way, striving to understand how each area and color should react to different lighting conditions. Ultimately, this results in a painting with consistent lighting, leading to a realistic and highly readable effect. Of course, after years of experience, you won't need to follow these steps in order—it will become second nature—but explaining the process this way makes it clearer.

THE ART DIRECTOR'S BRIEF

Before starting a digital painting, it's good to know where you're heading, except, of course, if it's a personal project. But when working in video games or film production, it's essential to try to understand and anticipate what your client or Art Director desires as a result. Your client has an image in mind when giving you a brief. Your goal is to get as close as possible to that image. Therefore, it's crucial to ask as many questions as possible during this meeting because you're dealing with a still abstract image. For example, you need to know the mood they imagine. Is it a scene that takes place during the day or at night? In the morning or evening? Is the sky cloudy, are the colors vibrant? Is it warm or gloomy? Do they have a particular stylization in mind? A film reference? What do they find important in the reference images they show you? What is the purpose of this image? Is it to design a particular element? Inspire the team? Provide lighting instructions? See the character in action in a certain setting? Dress up a level design? It's better to ask more questions than not enough. Sometimes you'll be surprised by the answers! The thing to absolutely avoid is realizing after the initial sketches that you didn't understand something crucial. It wastes time, and nobody likes that.

FIGURE 5.4 Asking the Art Director questions about the mood and the purpose of the painting helps to make the best choices from the start (digital painting done in Photoshop for *Assassin's Creed III* (*Assassin's Creed* TM & © Ubisoft Entertainment. All Rights Reserved).

FIGURE 5.5 Having to redo this painting with bright sunlight and a blue sky would take a lot of time to do. Asking the right questions even before starting is crucial (digital painting done in Photoshop over a game screenshot for *For Honor* (© Ubisoft Entertainment. All Rights Reserved).

VISUAL REFERENCES RESEARCH

Researching references is a crucial step that should never be neglected. You might have to spend hours just to ensure you have everything you need. Search for references for all the objects, buildings, vehicles, and characters that you will depict in your digital painting.

Sometimes, you need something very precise, from the right angle of view, and it can be challenging to find. Then, turn to 3D object sales sites because you can orbit around the object for sale. This allows you to find the perfect angle that will serve as a visual reference. It's very convenient.

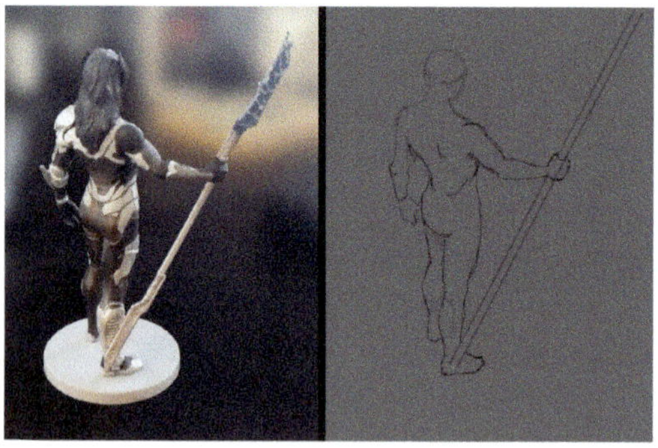

FIGURE 5.6 Don't hesitate to use toys as visual references for poses. Just take a picture from the right angle, with the right lens, it will help you a lot to draw with the correct perspective.

You can also search for pose references for your characters, so that the anatomy is as accurate as possible and the pose is interesting.

Additionally, look for images or paintings with atmospheres like those you want to represent. Set aside photos or paintings of skies that seem interesting to you for the image you need to create. Also, search for references of objects, textures, landscapes, and trees. The range is very wide.

Set aside film screenshots that are good references for the project you are working on.

Finally, collect images, paintings, or concept art from artists you admire, just to inspire you or to use a composition of an image that you find interesting for the work you must do. For a single digital painting, it's not uncommon to end up with hundreds of reference images.

THE BLANK CANVAS SYNDROME

This syndrome is indeed real. One can find themselves paralyzed by the infinite possibilities when faced with a blank canvas. The 'trick' to overcoming this syndrome is to immediately start drawing or painting something, a character silhouette, architecture, or anything related to what you want to paint.

FIGURE 5.7 Start with lines or shapes, anything that you can adjust and move around. Don't spend too long staring at a blank canvas—it might be intimidating and prevent you from starting something. Don't wait for inspiration; just show up and put yourself in a good state of mind. Inspiration will come when you are ready to embrace it.

You can also start with an existing illustration, painting, or image that may have no connection to the result except for something you like, such as a composition or color palette. Then, begin adding shapes, moving them around, duplicating others, etc. At least you're starting to work with something concrete, which allows you to compare, adjust, retouch, and add shapes. In this case, the anxiety of the blank canvas fades away very fast.

FIGURE 5.8A Starting from any image, select colors and values, and paint and/or move large shapes (digital painting done in Photoshop over a game screenshot for *Assassin's Creed Revelations* (*Assassin's Creed* TM & © Ubisoft Entertainment. All Rights Reserved).

FIGURE 5.8B Here is the result after a few minutes. You don't start from a blank canvas, and you can easily move things around to work on your composition.

THE INITIAL SKETCH

There isn't a single method for starting the initial sketches, and you can use different ones depending on the circumstances.

FIGURE 5.9A Here is an initial sketch done in a few minutes. It's just about throwing ideas on a canvas and playing with the shapes and the composition. Then you try to find good references for what you need (buildings, animals, props, etc.).

First, you can start with a quick line drawing to begin placing the different shapes on your canvas and see how you can organize your composition (see Figure 5.7). This only takes a few minutes, so don't hesitate to select parts of your sketch, move them, erase them, or redo them. This is a stage where you try to clarify what you have in mind. It's also the time when you choose which camera angle will be most suitable for the situation. These initial sketches don't need to be perfect, as no one will see them. But it really helps to find directions and resolve problems early in the process, which can save a considerable amount of time. In fact, it's better to realize a composition problem after a few minutes of doodling rather than after spending twenty hours on your digital painting.

FIGURE 5.9B Here is the result, after hours of work. The first sketch really helped to address problems early on, but you can see that it is still possible to make many changes during the process and to come up with new ideas for the composition (digital painting done in Photoshop for *Assassin's Creed Unity* (*Assassin's Creed* TM & © Ubisoft Entertainment. All Rights Reserved).

STARTING BY SKETCHING BIG LIGHT AND SHADOW SHAPES

This method is about sketching with shapes rather than lines. The goal is the same: Identify problems early on. The difference is that you can also start to think about your lighting and your value design (see chapter 3). You play with a few values (between two and four) and try to create an interesting composition with this additional parameter. This method can complement the first, as it can be used at a later stage. It is more relevant to cases where you are working on a personal digital painting or exploring ideas for a future game or movie. The goal is to have fun and create the most beautiful image possible without being limited by a specific subject. At this stage, you can work more freely and play with shapes, arranging them in an interesting and pleasing way. It's a fun way to work and can lead to interesting results. It's a bit like looking at clouds and seeing shapes that remind you of a character or an animal. The process is simple—you experiment as much as possible and hope for happy accidents that guide you in one direction or another. You can work with strong contrasts (painting in opaque black and white) or in color; it doesn't matter. There are no rules—what's important is that the image is interesting to look at, regardless of the subject matter.

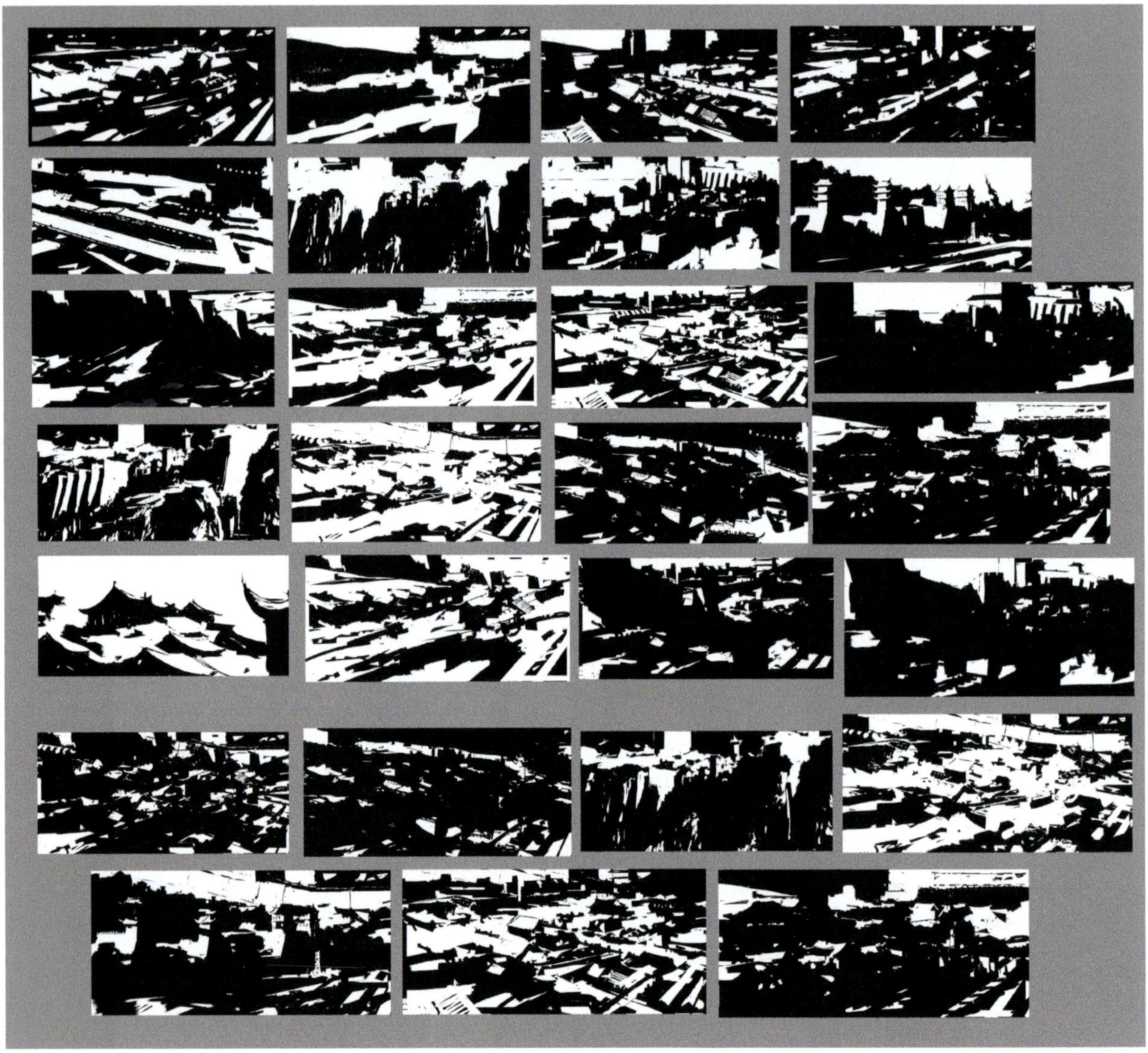

FIGURE 5.10A Here is a series of sketches done using only an opaque brush and two values. Try to focus on the harmony of the proportions between dark and light shapes. Then, a subject can appear, and you can refine the shapes, so they make more sense. It is a very fun and creative way of working (digital paintings done in Photoshop for *For Honor* (© Ubisoft Entertainment. All Rights Reserved).

Experiment with as many things as you can—distort, flip the image, crop, play with layer modes and opacity. Copy small parts of the image and distort them, and so on. Think a bit like a sculptor who just wants to sculpt without having a specific outcome in mind. You play with a block of clay, reshape it, cut it, lengthen it, flatten it, until something emerges. This is a super fun way of working, and it is not often useful during production, but very liberating when used.

FIGURE 5.10B Sketch done using only two values and an opaque brush, envisioning a gigantic fantasy fortress inspired by Chinese architecture. It has been done within a few minutes (as seen in Figure 5.10a, a lot of those were done, and this one was chosen to go further).

FIGURE 5.10C The final result. Adding details, colors, buildings in the shadow and refining shapes. The result is still sketchy but clear enough to illustrate an idea (Digital painting done in Photoshop for *For Honor* (© Ubisoft Entertainment. All Rights Reserved).

FOCUSING ON LIGHT VERSUS SHADOWS

Don't fall in love too quickly with one of your resulting compositions. Save ten or even twenty of them before deciding to keep one and push it further. It is preferable to carry out this process while working in a small format (1000 pixels wide at most). Focus on the big shapes and the abstract quality of your digital painting. It should catch the eye even when seen from afar. Try this technique—guaranteed enjoyment!

FIGURE 5.11A Here is an example of an interesting result you can get from focusing on the design between the light shapes and the dark shapes (digital painting done in Photoshop for *Assassin's Creed Valhalla* (*Assassin's Creed* TM & © Ubisoft Entertainment. All Rights Reserved).

FIGURE 5.11B Here is the thought behind it. The darker shapes form one big, unified shape, while the lighter shapes guide the viewer's eye toward the two main points of interest: the character and the landmark.

THE IMPORTANCE OF SHADOW SHAPES

Painting can seem a bit overwhelming; there are so many things to consider! As a result, it's not uncommon to feel a little lost, especially when you are a beginner and absorbing many new theoretical concepts. One thing that can help is to focus on the shape of the things you want to paint, and what defines the shape of these things is most often the shape of their shadows and their cast shadows. This is because your brain is trained to decipher shapes by analyzing the shape of shadows. So, if you concentrate on the shapes of these shadows, you will feel as though the subject of your painting appears as if by magic.

FIGURE 5.12A Painting without clear shadow information makes the artwork difficult to read.

FIGURE 5.12B Adding the shadow shapes makes the forms make sense, and the painting can now be read.

DESIGN WITH FOUR SIMPLE SHAPES

When you observe nature, you realize that you could recreate almost any object with just four simple shapes: the sphere, the cube, the cone, and the cylinder. These shapes are also called *primitives* in any 3D software. Of course, it is not about using these shapes only in their pure state; a sphere or a cube can be deformed or have different proportions. But the idea of having these shapes in mind when designing something is important.

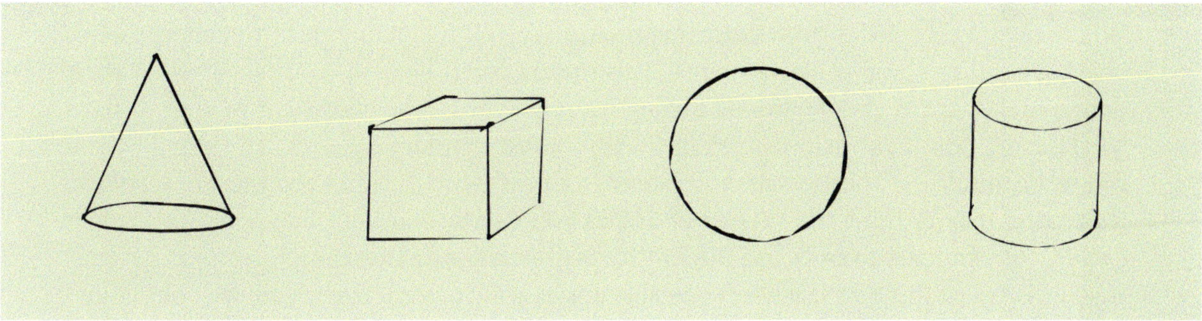

FIGURE 5.13 The four different primitive shapes you can choose from when designing something.

It's important to understand that your brain is naturally wired to assess potential threats by interpreting shapes in your surroundings. For instance, sharp or pointed forms often trigger a sense of caution—they're visually associated with danger. In contrast, rounder, softer shapes tend to feel safe, even comforting. While this isn't a strict rule, it reflects a deep-seated pattern in how you subconsciously process and respond to visual cues in your environment. In this way, when you have an object, a character, a building or a vehicle to design, it is good to think about these notions and not hesitate to play with them. For example, if you must design something related to the dark or evil forces of a game or a movie, you would probably favor straight, cubic, and pointed shapes. If, on the other hand, you must design a place or an object that must be reassuring or comforting, for example, for a children's game or movie, you would prioritize rounder shapes, at least you would use them mostly, perhaps even unconsciously. Obviously, this is by no means a rule; you just need to know that the viewer or the gamer, depending on the case, will recognize these codes because his brain works like this. On the other hand, it is good to try to play with these rules, and the results can be very interesting.

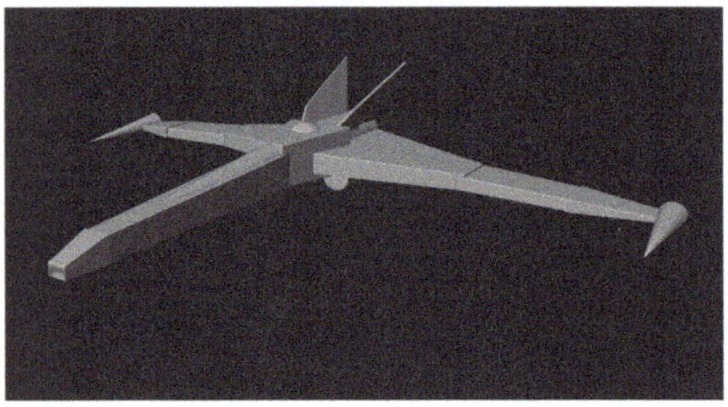

FIGURE 5.14A A first design example with a choice of more aggressive shapes mainly (squares, cones). You can add a few cylinders and spheres to complete it, but they must remain in the minority.

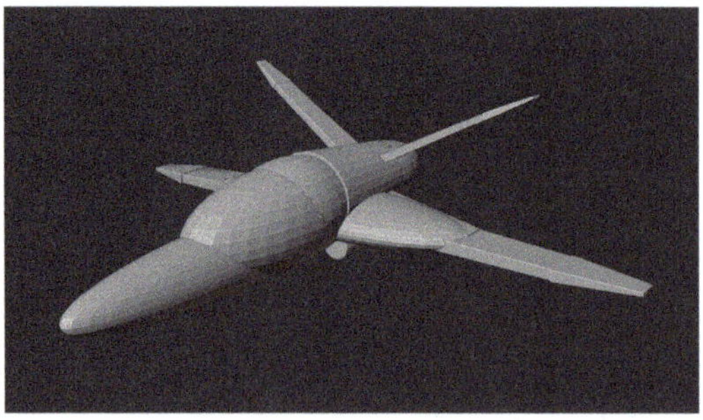

FIGURE 5.14B For the same type of vehicle to design, choosing rounder primitives gives a much more harmless feeling, making it look more like a transport jet than a combat jet. The same principle can be applied to the design of a building or a character.

DESIGN PRINCIPLES

When creating a setting from your imagination, you'll inevitably need to conceptualize objects, buildings, and other elements. This means you'll have to consider whether their design makes sense. As mentioned earlier, it's important to be consistent in your designs by choosing dominant primitive shapes (cube, cone, cylinder, sphere). Additionally, you should be mindful of the message you intend to convey with the lines you use. For instance, it's a good idea to limit the variety of angles you use to maintain harmony. You might decide, for example, to only use 90 and 45-degree angles in your architectural designs. If you disregard this and use every possible angle, your design might end up looking disjointed and hard to interpret. It is like limiting the number of values or colors you use, selecting specific ones to create pleasing harmonies is key. Like in music, if you press all the keys on a piano at once, the sound won't be harmonious.

FIGURE 5.15A Here is an example of a design for a simple prop that could easily be improved.

FIGURE 5.15B Indeed, if you carefully examine the angles, you'll notice that there are many different types, without any apparent justification. Observe how the green, blue, orange, and purple angles are all slightly different.

FIGURE 5.15C You can thus decide, for example, to use only three different angle values (0°, 45°, and 90°).

FIGURE 5.15D The difference from the original is subtle, but it still gives the impression that the design feels more solid and, above all, more credible.

Therefore, you should carefully and consciously choose the language of shapes, angles, and lines you want to use. This is part of your job if you wish to create worlds for film or video games. Often, the Art Director will guide you on what they're looking for, but they always appreciate it when you can bring good ideas to the table.

DESIGN PROBLEMS TO AVOID

When you must design some element in your painting, be careful about how some of the main lines end. Indeed, if strong lines converge at random points on the object you're designing, it can draw the viewer's eye to those spots, making it difficult to 'read' the form of the object. To avoid this, it's important to 'break' the direction of those lines so that they finish in a harmonious way.

FIGURE 5.16A Here is an example of a design with the presence of 'pinches', which should mostly be avoided.

FIGURE 5.16B They can be seen more clearly here (blue circles); when so many lines converge at a single point, it can draw attention to areas that are not particularly interesting.

FIGURE 5.16C Here is a proposal to solve the problem, though there are certainly others. You should strive to find solutions that feel harmonious to you. This is where your artistic eye and designer talents come into play.

Also, to make the design of an object or building believable, it's important to keep in mind its feasibility of construction. Of course, you can exaggerate certain elements, especially when working on a science fiction or fantasy project, but it's always good to consider basic principles of fabrication and constructability. For example, having a solid foundation that appears wider and gives a sense of well-distributed weight is crucial. Also, avoid creating openings within curves, as these are very difficult to construct in real life.

Think as well about how curves will end, where they stop, and how they transition or conclude. Study design from *Star Wars*, *Lord of the Rings* or *Halo* to learn from them.

TECHNICS TO COLOR YOUR BLACK AND WHITE PAINTING

You might find yourself starting a concept in grayscale, either by choice or because it was requested, and needing to colorize it. This initial black and white version might be quite advanced, and you might not have the time to repaint it entirely with colors.

FIGURE 5.17A a black and white sketch that needed to be colorized (digital painting done in Photoshop for *Assassin's Creed Origins* (*Assassin's Creed* TM & © Ubisoft Entertainment. All Rights Reserved).

In this case, it's useful to have some techniques for adding color to your digital painting. Here are a few:

Photo filters:

This tool allows you to simulate a lens filter over your entire image. Choose a filter of the desired color and paint on the mask to reveal only the objects of that color.

FIGURE 5.17B You can apply a photo filter in the desired color over your black-and-white painting.

FIGURE 5.17C Let's apply a warm overall color to the painting.

FIGURE 5.17D You can then add other color filters and paint on their masks to make the colors appear in the desired areas.

FIGURE 5.17E You can add as many color filters as needed to create a variety.

Pick colors from a photo:

Choose a reference image and use the color picker to select the desired color. Be careful to choose colors that correspond to the values in your black and white painting.

Pick a value then add color:

To ensure you pick a color that corresponds to the value in your black and white sketch, pick a value first, then add color to this value. Be careful not to change the value when adding color. Paint with that.

The curve tool:

This tool allows you to control the reds, greens, and blues separately. If you decide to go with a warm main light source, start by increasing the reds and yellows and decrease the blues, masking all the parts in shadow. Then, repeat the operation by boosting the blues and lowering the warm colors, and this time mask what is in the light.

FIGURE 5.17F Select 'Curves' from this menu to apply it to your image.

FIGURE 5.17G Choose a color channel here (red, in this example).

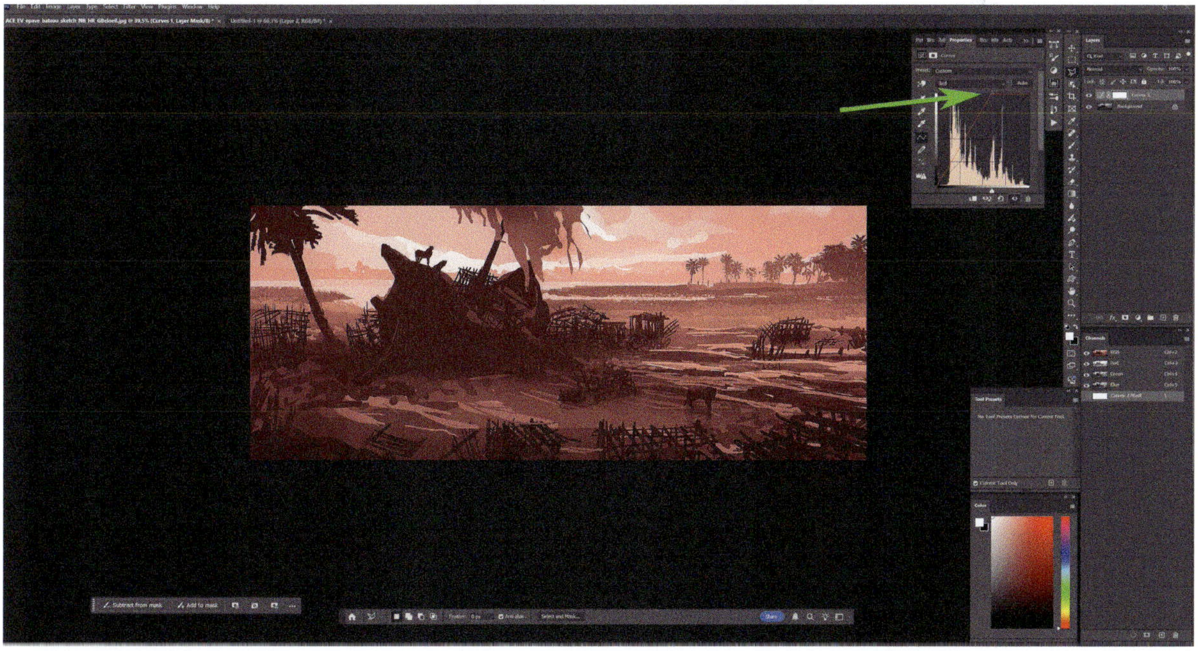

FIGURE 5.17H Adjust the settings—here, you can move this point to enhance the reds.

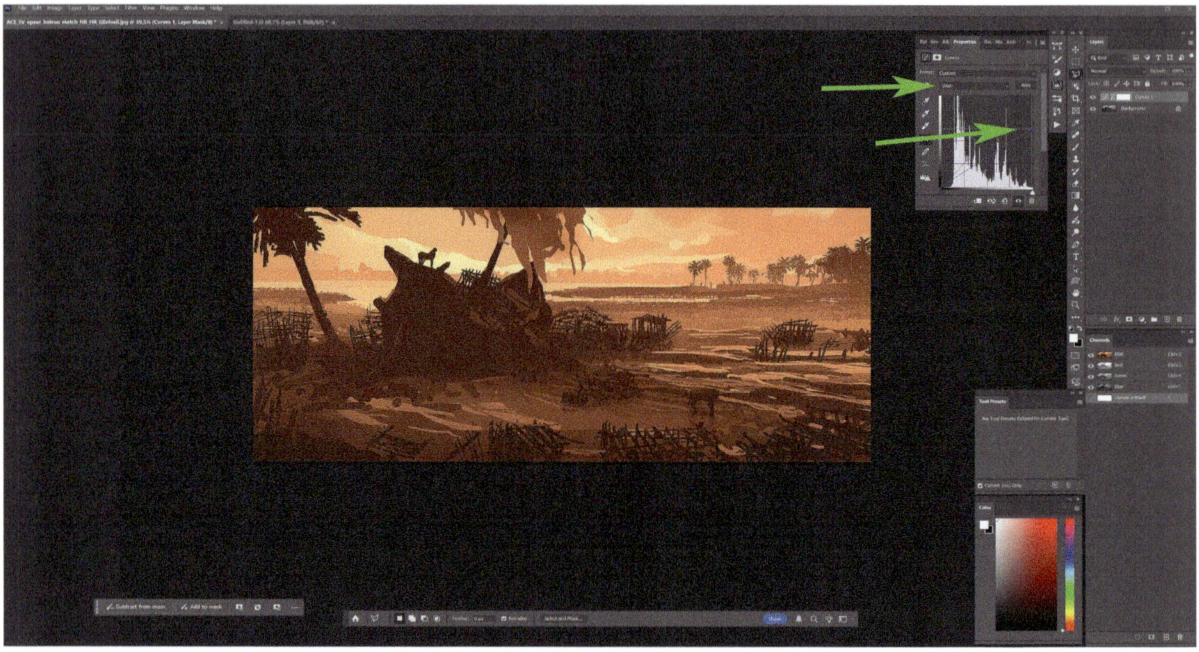

FIGURE 5.17I Now, select the blue channel and lower the point to bring out more yellows.

FIGURE 5.17J Then, paint on the mask to remove or add the desired color.

FIGURE 5.17K Repeat the process with additional 'Curves' layers to create new colors. Each time, paint on the masks to reveal the desired areas.

The image/adjustments/match color tool: This tool allows you to adjust the color palette of your painting to match another image's palette. Be careful, as values can be affected. To use this tool, your painting must be on a single layer (use copy merge/paste if needed). This process won't work if your painting is completely in grey scale, you need to have at least some sort of colors to start from.

FIGURE 5.17L First, add some color to your painting using any of the techniques presented earlier. You need to start with an image that contains color information to match it with another image colors. This tool does not work on grayscale images.

FIGURE 5.17M Now, copy/merge and paste over everything. The tool only works on a layer that contains information.

FIGURE 5.17N Make sure the layer with the colors you want to modify is selected, then apply the 'Match Colors' tool.

FIGURE 5.17O Now, you need to select the source image (and the correct layer) from the dropdown menu, which will serve as the color palette reference for your image.

FIGURE 5.17P Here is the result. Note that this works best when the values and colors of both images are already close or similar. Be aware that it's working better as a fine-tuning tool.

Of course, coloring a black and white sketch will require a combination of all these techniques. Use this process when you are short on time and don't have the option to color it instead of repainting it. But the result will never be as good as when you start directly in color or repaint everything from scratch, using your grayscale painting as a drawing reference.

FIGURE 5.17Q The final version, with a bit more details, colorized using the techniques described above (digital painting done in Photoshop for *Assassin's Creed Origins* (*Assassin's Creed* TM & © Ubisoft Entertainment. All Rights Reserved).

HOW TO START YOUR PAINTING DIRECTLY INTO COLORS

Sometimes, you might have trouble matching the mood and colors of your digital painting with the references provided by the Art Director. A lot of different methods exist; here is one of them that works.

This is a technique that allows you to work immediately with the right color palette or at least have a harmonious color scheme as a starting point. For this, it is better to have a clear idea of your objective, with a solid drawing base. This could be a line drawing, a 3D wireframe, or even a black-and-white sketch on which you've applied a *glowing edges* filter.

FIGURE 5.18A Here is the starting point. Instead of colorizing it, if you have time, the best approach is to repaint it entirely, using this black-and-white version only as a drawing reference.

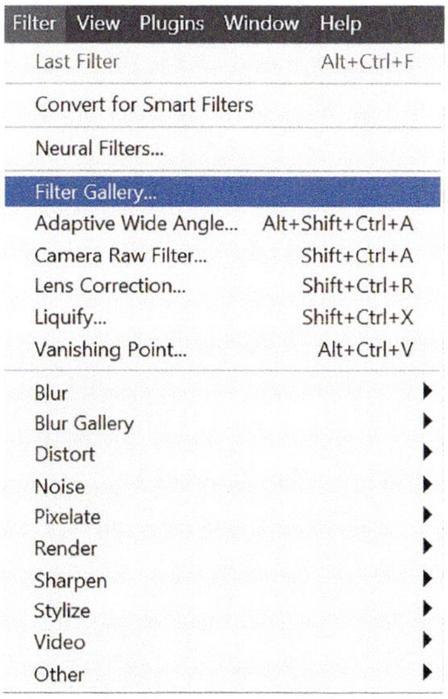

FIGURE 5.18B In the 'Filter' menu, choose 'Filter Gallery'.

FIGURE 5.18C In the 'Stylize' folder, you can find the 'Glowing Edges' filter. Click it and adjust the settings to get the clearest drawing possible from your painting.

Set the layer with this drawing to *multiply* or *screen* mode, depending on whether your image is light or dark.

FIGURE 5.18D You should end up with a result like this.

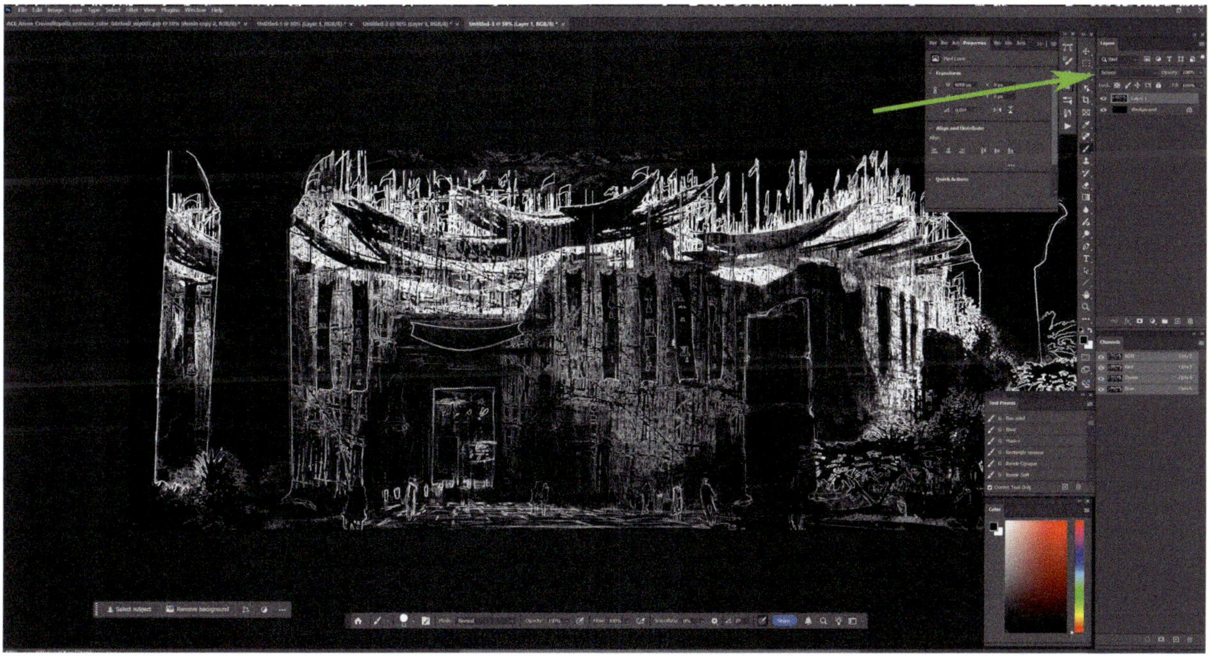

FIGURE 5.18E Set the layer with this image to 'Screen' mode so it becomes transparent, except for the light lines.

On the layer below, place your image, painting, or photo that will be your starting point. Logically, this image will have been provided by your client or Art Director as a reference for the desired mood or colors. Now you can start painting shapes based on your initial drawing. You pick the colors and values you think are appropriate and define your shapes. By starting with this image, you ensure you are heading in the right direction from the beginning of the process, and the result can be very quickly interesting.

FIGURE 5.18F Insert your reference image, with the correct color palette, beneath the 'drawing' layer.

FIGURE 5.18G Now you can start painting by selecting colors from your reference image and following the lines and shapes visible in your drawing.

FIGURE 5.18H After a while, your painting should look like this. You'll need your drawing less as a reference.

FIGURE 5.18I You can now add details and shapes that weren't even in your original sketch.

FIGURE 5.18J The final result (digital painting done in Photoshop for *Assassin's Creed Origins* (*Assassin's Creed* TM & © Ubisoft Entertainment. All Rights Reserved).

If it's a personal project and/or mood exploration, you can use the same drawing and start with images that have completely different palettes and moods. This will allow you to see which direction your digital painting should take to achieve the most interesting result.

As we'll explore later in this book, nothing prevents you from adjusting colors and lighting down the line—but starting with strong color harmony gives you a solid foundation. This is a very practical and effective method. Test it to see what you can get out of it.

STARTING FROM AN EXISTING IMAGE

As seen earlier to avoid the blank canvas syndrome (Figures 5.6a and 5.6b), a method you can use is to start with an existing image, photo, or painting related to the desired result. For example, starting to paint over a visual reference that the Art Director likes. This can be a good way to begin a sketch, especially when colors are an important part of the concept. Obviously, the goal is to play with, move shapes, subtract, or add to achieve a different result, but it can be an interesting starting point.

FIGURE 5.19A "Vladimirka", a painting by Isaac Levitan (1892).

FIGURE 5.19B Pick a guide as a drawing (it can be 3D or a sketch done with shapes) with a composition that seems to be a good starting point, set to a layer in 'multiply' or 'screen' mode, to paint your own image using the palette from the painting above.

FIGURE 5.19C Resize the image to fit the required aspect ratio. Use it as a palette to pick colors and values. It doesn't have to be a painting; you can also start from a photo.

FIGURE 5.19D It doesn't matter if the subject of the painting is completely different; You just focus on selecting the colors and values.

FIGURE 5.19E Now that you're satisfied with the overall colors and values, you can focus on adding details and making this painting more readable.

FIGURE 5.19F Don't hesitate to change the color palette during the process. The important thing is that you started with a solid color harmony. The painting was just the starting point.

FIGURE 5.19G Compared to the starting image, you can see that it is now a completely different painting, but it helped you to begin with something strong.

STARTING WITH A DETAILED DRAWING

If you are comfortable with line drawing, it's a good idea to start your painting by maximizing the quality of the drawing. This will allow you to use it as a solid foundation for your painting, ensuring that your digital artwork has a strong base. You can then fully focus on the values and color harmonies. A high-quality and detailed base drawing is almost a guarantee of success for the result.

FIGURE 5.20A You can spend time on a hand drawing to ensure it will serve as a solid guide for your painting.

FIGURE 5.20B You just must invert the layer with the drawing and applied the 'screen' mode, allowing you to paint on one layer beneath it.

FIGURE 5.20C At this stage, you can toggle the drawing layer on and off. You would probably mostly be working without it at this point, as the overall shapes are established. Notice how you can adjust the color harmony—a process that's incredibly easy in digital painting but quite challenging with traditional media.

FIGURE 5.20D After hours of rendering, studying references, and striving to describe forms as accurately as possible, you shouldn't need the drawing; it is now solely about painting.

STARTING FROM SIMPLE 3D SHAPES

One method you can use is starting with a very simple 3D base as a drawing reference. You might use this method in situations where you must sketch a very complex architecture. Then, you use it as a drawing base and sketch from there. It is useful because you can easily play with the camera angle. If you think it's quicker for you to place a few models in 3D software than to draw them by hand, you shouldn't hesitate to do it. You should always try to choose the method that best suits the situation.

FIGURE 5.21A Start with a simple 3d model. Just make a screenshot and open it in Photoshop.

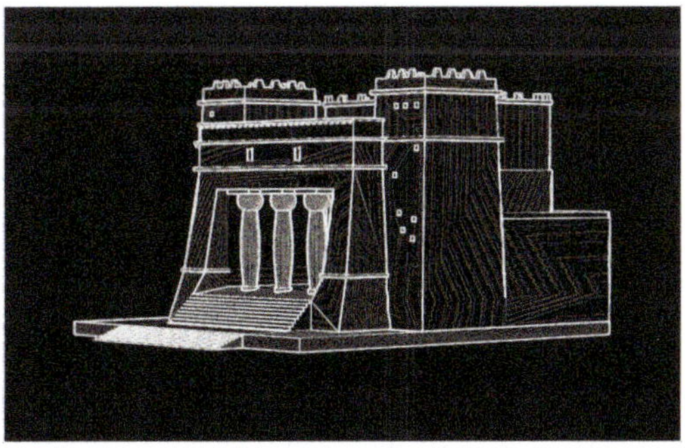

FIGURE 5.21B Apply the 'Glowing Edges' filter to transform the image into a drawing-like effect.

FIGURE 5.21C Set the layer to 'Screen' mode, and paint on a new layer in 'Normal' mode, using the previous layer as a drawing reference.

FIGURE 5.21D For the result, you don't need to render the 3D model. Just use it as a drawing reference and paint.

As already mentioned, if you need to add one specific element in your digital painting, simply take a screenshot of an existing 3D object from an online marketplace and use it as a drawing guide. For instance, you can use Sketchfab for this purpose, as one can preview a model, rotate it, and even play with the lighting. It's a great way to get a precise visual reference from the right angle to paint from. (https://sketchfab.com/)

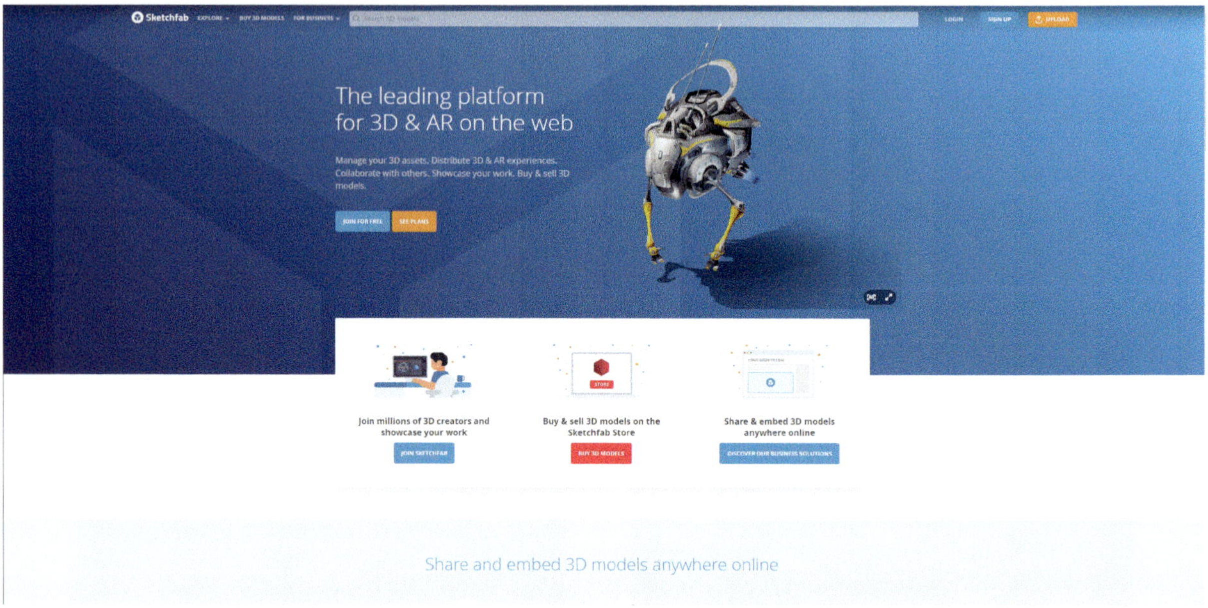

FIGURE 5.21E Sketchfab interface, a great way to get some precise visual references.

UTILIZATION OF A MORE COMPLEX 3D SCENE

It is difficult today to completely avoid using 3D to create a digital painting for concept art in video games or films because Art Directors like to have something close to the final product (the game or the film), and with increasingly powerful graphics cards, the results are becoming more realistic, especially regarding materials and lighting. However, it is still possible to work without using 3D. Indeed, if you are working on an extremely stylized image for a cartoon or a very cartoonish video game, strong drawing skills will suffice. On the other hand, for a more realistic digital painting with architecture, it would be a shame to miss out on the help of 3D software, and it is a good thing that you at least know the basics as it can really save you a lot of time. Today, Blender is the most popular software, but things evolved quickly. The good news is that 3D software is becoming easier to learn and use. In the early 2000s, you really had to take a course or read books on specific software, buy a very expensive computer, and the software was really complicated to learn and use (and super expensive as well). Today, resources are free, the software is very user-friendly, and it is open source, which means you can acquire upgrades that suit your needs at a very low price.

You can use 3D in different ways. The first is that you will quickly place shapes, take a screenshot, and use the result as a kind of guide for your drawing, especially to guide the perspective. (See the previous part about 'the initial sketches' (Figures 5.21a–5.21d).)

You can also push the 3D a bit further to get more precision but can still use it as a drawing reference only.

FIGURE 5.22A For more complicated architecture at a difficult angle, it's better to push the 3D modeling a bit further. It is not necessary to spend time on textures and lighting; You just need a good drawing reference.

FIGURE 5.22B Since the 3D model contains plenty of detail and interesting shapes, it's a good idea to take advantage of it by producing a simplified render with only two values. This type of render can then be used in Photoshop as a selection base, making it easier to paint precise shapes.

FIGURE 5.22C Try moving the key light to create interesting angles—coming from above, below, the right, or the left. Again, use it as a selection base in Photoshop to help you paint shapes. You might not end up using all the shapes it reveals, but chances are you'll find a few that work well.

FIGURE 5.22D You can then apply the 'glowing edges' filter on Figure 5.22a in Photoshop to create a drawing from this 3D render.

FIGURE 5.22E Start to paint with the needed color palette, using the line drawing (Figure 5.22d) as a guide and the selections you got from Figure 5.22b and Figure 5.22c, to paint nice and clean shapes.

FIGURE 5.22F You can see it is possible to add a lot of things that were not in the 3D render and that is fine, just paint them. The goal is just to use the 3D as a guide to start from (digital painting done in Photoshop with a 3D render as a guide, *Assassin's Creed Valhalla* (*Assassin's Creed* TM & © Ubisoft Entertainment. All Rights Reserved).

PAINT OVER A 3D RENDER

This is the most time-consuming method: You push the 3D as far as possible, applying textures, lighting, and rendering to create a highly detailed base. From there, you paint over the result to enhance and refine the final image. This approach is ideal when aiming for photorealistic outcomes, especially in scenes featuring complex architectural elements. It's widely used in matte painting workflows, where artists begin with a fully realized 3D render and then modify and paint over it in Photoshop to achieve a polished, cinematic result.

FIGURE 5.23A The starting point: a highly detailed 3D render. It takes time to construct such a scene, but if you need a photorealistic look, it might be the way to start.

FIGURE 5.23B The final result after finishing it in Photoshop. No brushstrokes should be visible to get a photorealistic look.

USING PHOTOS

Photo bashing is a legitimate creative technique, and in fact, some Art Directors specifically require it. It involves using photographs, retouching them, and combining them to produce a photorealistic result—rich in detail and realism. Some artists truly excel at this method, and their work can be stunning. Despite what some may believe, photo bashing is not 'cheating'. It demands a strong grasp of fundamentals such as lighting and perspective, the ability to recognize different camera lenses, and the skill to paint in or modify elements with accuracy and artistic intention. Those who excel at photo bashing are often well-rounded artists. If you want to get into this way of working, you must have a solid grasp of all the fundamentals mentioned in this book; otherwise, your work may not meet your expectations.

Also, be mindful of copyright concerns when using photos. Whenever possible, use your own images, or be sure to blend at least three photos from different photographers. This helps ensure that no one feels their work has been misused and that the result is genuinely yours. Alternatively, you can use photo bashing more subtly—just to add specific details or to help block out shapes like buildings or landscapes. Eventually, you'll paint over those sections so extensively that the original photo will nearly vanish. We'll take a closer look at this technique later in Chapter 6.

Sometimes, you might use a photo to trace a shape you want to be realistic or simply to help you find interesting shapes, values, or color variations by playing with happy accidents that can occur. You can also use photos to create montages that you trace to paint from accurate shapes. Like in the following example:

FIGURE 5.24A Here is a photo to start from.

FIGURE 5.24B You can flip the picture horizontally if needed and add parts of movie screenshots and photos to create a montage with all the elements you need. At this point, focus on the composition, scale, and perspective. Make sure that the lenses used for each picture seemed similar. You can also quickly paint over some parts to help you achieve the vision you have in mind.

FIGURE 5.24C When you're happy with the result, apply a 'glowing edges' filter in Photoshop to create a sort of drawing from your montage. This will now serve as the line drawing from which you will paint. It's time to refine the drawing if needed.

FIGURE 5.24D You now begin to apply values and colors to set the mood you envision.

FIGURE 5.24E Do not hesitate to repaint from scratch some parts or even the entire image. From this moment on, you interact with the painting (the drawing is not needed anymore) and try to solve any problems you notice.

FIGURE 5.24F Add details, texture, and light. You might need to change some designs to make it as interesting as possible.

To conclude, and as already mentioned, the best would be to start with a solid drawing, a 3D model or a photo; it's not important how. Starting with a good line art is the safer way to succeed.

CALL-OUTS

Just for your information—and this is something more specific to environment concept art—an Art Director may sometimes ask you to be more precise about an object by requesting what's called a 'call-out'. This is a separate drawing or painting that provides additional detail and clarity about the object's form and components. Of course, the same techniques apply to paint those elements.

FIGURE 5.25A Following this concept art, it has been asked to create *call-outs* to describe more precisely the elements that make up the bridge (digital painting done in Photoshop over a game screenshot for *Assassin's Creed Valhalla* (*Assassin's Creed* TM & © Ubisoft Entertainment. All Rights Reserved).

FIGURE 5.25B Here is the details of the pillars to help 3D artists construct these objects (digital paintings done in Photoshop for *Assassin's Creed Valhalla* (*Assassin's Creed* TM & © Ubisoft Entertainment. All Rights Reserved).

FIGURE 5.25C Here is another detail describing how these pillars work and what the special effects should look like (digital paintings done in Photoshop for *Assassin's Creed Valhalla* (*Assassin's Creed* TM & © Ubisoft Entertainment. All Rights Reserved).

FIGURE 5.25D And finally, another detail: the connection between the bridge and the world of Asgard, along with visual intentions for the special effects as well. (Digital paintings done in Photoshop for *Assassin's Creed Valhalla* (*Assassin's Creed* TM & © Ubisoft Entertainment. All Rights Reserved).

FIGURE 6.1 Digital painting done in Photoshop for *Assassin's Creed Origins* (*Assassin's Creed* TM & © Ubisoft Entertainment. All Rights Reserved).

CHAPTER 6

Finishing Your Digital Painting

DOI: 10.1201/9781003536703-7

This is a phase that should not be started too early. Indeed, you must be sure that everything is in place: the composition, the drawing, the values, and the colors before you begin to detail and finalize your digital painting. Unfortunately, you'll probably fall into the trap of detailing things in your painting instead of focusing on the fundamentals. You'll do that because it's easier, more satisfying, and it does help enhance the visual quality of your painting—at least most of the time. In fact, it will only delay the inevitable and ultimately waste your time, increasing the visual quality of your image by maybe 10%, not more.

You need to work smarter, and before jumping into the details, don't hesitate to completely repaint parts of the image, or even most of it. If you've spent two hours detailing a character or a spaceship in a part of your image, you might become emotionally attached and find it hard to erase that part, even if you realize something isn't working. Try not to finalize your painting until you are certain everything works correctly, or until your client gives you the green light to do so. But it's not easy to discipline yourself to this extent, and it is easy to fall into the trap of painting details too early in the process. Be smarter in your approach, and you will save a lot of time and avoid unnecessary frustrations.

Now, let's imagine you made sure everything is in place, and your painting appears solid in terms of its fundamentals, it's time to finalize.

BREAK STRAIGHT LINES AND FLAT SURFACES

This is one of the first things you should do to finalize your digital painting. Often, especially if you're starting from a 3D render, you'll notice the presence of perfect or at least uninterrupted lines in your image, as well as flat areas. When you spot them, a red flag should immediately go up in your mind. You need to act. Look for opportunities to break these lines, often by adding geometry. Try to find the right solutions—what object could potentially break this line? This is where your imagination or common sense comes into play.

FIGURE 6.2A Observe the outline of the two main towers. You can see that the lines are continuous and appear unnatural. This kind of clean lines should always raise a red flag.

FIGURE 6.2B A minimal amount of work is enough to break these lines. You can imagine adding geometric elements that make sense, so the silhouette of the two towers appears more natural. The difference is subtle but very important for the result.

ADDING DETAILS AND/OR VARIATIONS

Indeed, you might find that some parts seem a bit too vague or some edges are too messy. This is the moment to spend time in these areas. You don't have to add details everywhere. There should be variation: Some parts are very detailed, others less so. These parts are chosen based on distance, focus points, or their interest in storytelling. Finalizing doesn't just mean adding details; it means clearly defining shapes and adding variations in some parts that might be too uniform. Defining shapes means asking yourself what the primitive shape you want to represent is. Is it more of a sphere? A cube? A cylinder? Once you have clearly defined this shape, you can then focus on its realization. For example, if it's a spherical shape, see if you can correct its roundness to make it more accurate. Use the ellipse selection tool to help with this.

FIGURE 6.3A Here is an example of shapes that lack definition. When you zoom in on your digital painting, you will likely notice some areas that are a bit too imprecise—sections painted quickly that don't quite capture the shapes you had in mind. When you're at the final stage, it's time to refine and clean up those shapes.

FIGURE 6.3B Using selection tools is a good way to clean up the edges, and you can also define the shape more precisely within the selection.

FIGURE 6.3C Finishing your painting is mainly about cleaning up the edges and defining your shapes better.

PLAY WITH COLOR TEMPERATURES

If the shape is well-defined, you can now add color temperature variations. These can be subtle but will help your painting appear richer and more interesting to look at. Indeed, when you're nearing the end of the process, it's a good idea to play with varying the differences in color temperatures here and there. Try to do it logically, but not exclusively. Having areas where the colors warm up and cool down subtly will add visual richness and additional interest for the viewer. As you already saw, Monet played a lot with this aspect. Don't hesitate to experiment with this, and to do so, you can use the *curves* and *photo filter* tools as follows:

FIGURE 6.4A Here is an opportunity to vary the color temperature a bit to bring warmth to certain parts.

FIGURE 6.4B You can choose a 'Photo Filter' layer, but you can use other methods, such as a 'Curves' layer or painting the desired color directly. The important thing is to be able to adjust the color temperature.

FIGURE 6.4C If you need more warmth, you can apply an orange tint and can adjust the intensity of the effect.

FIGURE 6.4D Now, fill the mask with black so that the layer effect is no longer visible.

FIGURE 6.4E The last step is to paint white on the mask to reveal the areas where you want warmer colors. It now looks richer in terms of colors.

DEFINE AREAS AS IF THEY WERE DIFFERENT TINY COMPOSITIONS

Another thing: Try to consider each part of your painting as separate small compositions and try to give each an interest. Sometimes, to help you do this, you can create a frame within the image and approach what's inside this frame as another painting with its own composition and interest.

FIGURE 6.5A Let's say you want to refine this painting (digital painting done in Photoshop for *Assassin's Creed Unity* (*Assassin's Creed* TM & © Ubisoft Entertainment. All Rights Reserved).

FIGURE 6.5B You can use this cropping technique and consider all these small compositions as paintings.

FIGURE 6.5C Now focus on another part. It's a very effective method for finalizing digital painting.

This can really help make your digital painting more visually interesting and encourage viewers to spend more time looking at your work. Admire and study the work of Craig Mullins in this regard; he is a master at this (https://www.goodbrush.com/).

PASTE PHOTOS WHEN YOU ARE STUCK

Sometimes, a part of your digital painting seems to lack something. Variation, interesting shapes, a different arrangement of values, or simple details. In this case, you can copy/paste a photo onto this part. Generally, this photo is related to the subject, but it is not mandatory. You can then play with the *opacity* of the layer and sometimes even with the *mode* of its application. Your goal is to find 'happy accidents' that will help you unlock this problem. When you see something interesting, paint over it, keeping only the shapes/colors/values that interest you. This is interesting because it really brings surprising results. Of course, experience helps in using it correctly, but that comes with time. In fact, this practice is certainly one of the big advantages of working digitally.

FIGURE 6.6A In this example, let's add some details to the village seen in the distance. Let's paste a photo there to help.

FIGURE 6.6B As you can see, the subject of the photo is very similar to that of this digital painting, though that doesn't necessarily have to be the case. The goal is to find happy accidents to help unlock a situation. Start to experiment with different layer blending modes to try to find something visually interesting.

FIGURE 6.6C Let's choose the 'Multiply' mode for this example and let's adjust the layer opacity until the desired effect is achieved.

FIGURE 6.6D Then, mask this layer and unmask the parts that interest you the most by painting with white.

FIGURE 6.6E Finally, create a new layer on top and paint by picking the colors that interest you. Clean up the shapes, refine some of them, and create new ones.

EDGES

What is called *edge* is the area that separates two shapes of different values. The theory and practice concerning *edges* are often poorly understood or ignored in the world of concept art or digital painting. It must be said that many artists deal very intuitively with this notion, without necessarily knowing the theory behind it.

To realize the importance of the quality of *edges* in digital painting, you can do this very enlightening exercise: study an image, painting, or photo with a simple 100% opaque brush and observe the result. You will immediately notice that your painting seems extremely simplistic, and the shapes are difficult to define correctly.

FIGURE 6.7A Here is an example of a study done with a 100% opaque brush, primarily using hard edges. The result is clearly neither realistic nor satisfying. It is almost impossible to accurately describe the roundness of certain shapes.

Second, introduce different qualities of *edges* and see the difference.

FIGURE 6.7B The same digital painting, but this time with refined edges. Notice how the difference is huge—it instantly looks more realistic.

Thus, you could divide these edges qualities into four distinct categories:

- **Hard edge:** This is the one you just used with this opaque brush. The boundary between the shapes is clear, the contrast is very strong. Ideally, you will not use or very little of this kind of *edge*. If necessary, you will use it at the focal point of your painting, where the light strikes hard and where the contrasts of value are important. If you use too much of this kind of *edge*, your digital painting becomes difficult to read.

FIGURE 6.8 In this painting, notice that the harder edges are located on the head of the character on the left, which immediately draws the viewer's attention (*The Fountain, Villa Torlonia, Frascati, Italy*, painted by John Singer Sargent in 1907).

- **Firm edge:** The contrast remains important, but lesser. You also use it in lit areas to describe abrupt changes in angle of form, without it becoming glaring and aggressive.

FIGURE 6.9 Here is an example of a firm edge. You can sense that the described shape transitions abruptly from light to shadow, but it is not contrasted or sharp enough to draw the viewer's eye (*Self-portrait with a Model*, Anders Zorn, 1896).

- **Soft edge:** The most common. You could make a painting with just this type of *edge*. John Singer Sargent once said that there was no such thing as *hard edge* in real life, only *soft edges*. It is better to use it to the maximum if you want your painting to be pleasant to look at. Sargent and Velasquez were masters of *edge* control; you should try to observe their paintings closely to realize this. The way they played with the variation of edge quality was perfect. Notice that there are no such things as hard edges in shadow, so always use *soft edges* or *lost edges* to paint shapes in shadow.

FIGURE 6.10 In this painting, notice the quality of the edges, particularly the soft edges around the contours of the arm. This creates the impression that it is in motion and helps indicate that the form is rounded, rather than stopping abruptly, as a hard edge would suggest (*Sibyl with Tabula Rasa* by Diego Velázquez, 1648).

- **Lost edge:** The most fun, the most spectacular of *edge* types. To be used as soon as you have the opportunity, even if here again you should not abuse it so that your painting does not appear blurry. It is about making almost invisible the boundary between two values that are very similar. For example, in a portrait, the shape of the hair that is lost in a dark background. In these circumstances, you will describe the shape simply by playing with the temperature of the colors. It's very powerful and viewers love it because they can finish some parts of the painting in their mind, and it's a very pleasant feeling for them.

FIGURE 6.11 There are many beautiful lost edges in this painting. You can see them where the green circles are placed, but also in the character's eyes, where the edges disappear completely between the pupil and the eyelashes. (*Carolus-Duran* (detail) by John Singer Sargent, 1879)

In conclusion, if you spend a little time taking care of the quality of the *edges* in your painting, the result can really take a beautiful turn, and this in a very short time. Unfortunately, this is an aspect that tends to be neglected, especially when in production and under tight deadlines. But you should spend some time on it if you can, the result is worth it.

WHEN DO YOU KNOW IT'S DONE?

This is the big question. Richard Schmid used to say that an artist needed another artist with a hammer standing behind him to knock him out at the right moment so he would stop and not ruin his painting.

Fortunately, in digital painting, you don't need that; indeed you always have the option to revert to a previous version if necessary. You can work indefinitely on the same painting without risk. But the question remains the same: When to stop?

When it's an image for a client or an Art Director, you try to do your best and show them work-in-progress versions regularly to get their feedback and ensure we're heading in the direction they want. You stop when they are fully satisfied. Easy.

FIGURE 6.12 Digital painting done in Photoshop.

However, when it's a personal project, the answer is more challenging. You obviously strive to create the best possible image, but before putting it in your portfolio, just wait a little bit. If you still think your painting holds up, let it rest a bit and look at it again. Chances are, you will see new things to correct that you have missed. Why? Because your brain, once again, plays tricks on you. It tends to 'correct' errors on its own before you do it! This is something to be aware of. You also need to consider that working on an image for too long can lead to a certain weariness, and you might unconsciously avoid seeing certain errors just to move on to something else.

To counter this, regularly use the horizontal flip (you can create a shortcut for it in Photoshop, so you can use it very often) and let the image rest for a few days when you think it's finished.

If after that, you believe your image is presentable and would be a good addition to your portfolio, it's probably finished. If it's personal work, you are the only judge. To paraphrase Alex Kanevsky: Don't take good or bad critics from others too seriously, have confidence in yourself, convince yourself that you are a great artist, but be your harshest critic.

At the same time, sometimes you can be too harsh on yourselves, and you might realize, after looking at your painting several days later, that it was better than you initially thought. This happens frequently when you have high standards for yourself.

FIGURE 6.13 A digital painting that appears to be finished, with enough details. (Digital painting done in Photoshop for the game *Assassin's Creed Origins* (*Assassin's Creed* TM & © Ubisoft Entertainment. All Rights Reserved).

THE LAST 10% REWARD

As mentioned earlier, after spending hours on a digital painting, it's easy to grow tired of looking at it. At some point, you may feel like you've reached the finish line—or at least can't see how to improve it further. It's rare to feel truly satisfied with your own work. There's always a vision in your mind of what you hoped to achieve, and often, the result falls short of that ideal.

Eventually, fatigue and frustration take over. You sense the painting is nearly done, and so you stop—partly out of weariness. You still notice areas that could be improved, but you're simply too drained to keep going. So, you leave it as is.

It's a mistake.

When you revisit artworks you once considered finished—when you truly push yourself to refine them further (assuming you have the time, which isn't always possible in a production setting)—the results can be well worth the effort. You might be surprised by how much a painting can improve and reach a whole new level.

That's why it's often worth continuing, even when you think you're done. Push just 10% further, and the results may surprise and reward you. Try stepping away from your painting for a while and return to it with fresh eyes. You'll likely have the clarity and energy to repaint entire sections, elevating the artwork far beyond what you originally envisioned.

FIGURE 6.14A First version of this digital painting. At the time, the main character of the video game had not yet been designed, so he is painted as he appeared in the previous game (*Assassin's Creed Brotherhood*). The image seemed finished and was considered as such for months, until it was asked to repaint the character with his new design.

FIGURE 6.14B It was an opportunity to rework certain parts of the image in addition to the character, which made the painting look better. This is the benefit an extra 10% of time can have on a painting (*Assassin's Creed* TM & © Ubisoft Entertainment. All Rights Reserved).

ENTIRELY REPAINTING SOME PARTS

As seen in the previous example, it's necessary sometimes not to hesitate to repaint a whole part of your image. You must have the strength not to become emotionally attached to your painting and, above all, not to think about all the time you spent on this or that part. You need to have a cold eye and not hesitate to start over 100%. Moreover, considering that redoing a part that clearly doesn't work is often very rewarding. You work more quickly and simplify the shapes. This is because you know where you're going, and you don't go through the trial-and-error stages you've already been through. The result is often much better. It's also for the same reason that it's good to go through the sketch stage before tackling the main painting.

If you think that redoing part of a painting is a kind of admission of weakness, think of the great master of painting, John Singer Sargent, who didn't hesitate to redo a portrait twenty times (!) to achieve perfection. He also did it so that the result looked like it had been painted *du premier coup* (in one go), with bold and confident brushstrokes. If he found benefit in it, it's probably a good idea to do it. So don't hesitate, especially with digital, which always allows you to go back to a previous version, something traditional painting doesn't allow.

FIGURE 6.15 Beautiful portrait by Sargent, which he probably repainted multiple times to achieve complete satisfaction, yet it gives the impression that these confident brush strokes were placed perfectly on the first attempt (*Portrait of Violette Sargent* by John Singer Sargent, 1875).

CHECKLIST

When you notice something is wrong but can't quite identify the issue, try flipping your digital painting horizontally, as mentioned earlier. This can give you a fresh perspective. If the problem still isn't clear, it can help to go through this mental checklist:

- Are the values, okay? Can you differentiate between light and shadow? Do you get less contrast between lights and darks in the distance?
- Is the lighting consistent with the position of the light source?
- Is the value design (contrast between dark and light shapes) engaging? Can it be improved? Can you join some dark masses together? Can you join some light masses together? Can you use less values?

FIGURE 6.16 Digital painting done in Photoshop for *Assassin's Creed Syndicate* (*Assassin's Creed* TM & © Ubisoft Entertainment. All Rights Reserved).

- Does the atmospheric perspective feel sufficient, or can it be enhanced to create more depth?
- Are the shapes varied enough, or do they show repetitive patterns? Have you paid attention to the quality of negative shapes?
- Is the perspective accurate?
- Are the anatomy and poses of characters or creatures correct? Should you refer to references for improvement?
- Are the scale and proportions accurate? Stairs, windows and characters are good clues for scale. Check these out. Can the scale be exaggerated somewhere for added impact?

FIGURE 6.17 Digital painting done in Photoshop for *For Honor* (© Ubisoft Entertainment. All Rights Reserved).

- Have ellipses been painted? If so, are they accurate?
- Are there any tangents present? If so, can they be corrected by adding overlaps?
- Can overlapping be added to clarify the spatial relationship between shapes?
- Do lines or shapes appear to abruptly stop behind others? If so, extending those lines slightly can indicate that they pass behind the shape.
- Is the language of shapes, lines and angles in the designs of objects or buildings harmonious and consistent?
- Can more contrast be added (e.g., big/small, cool/warm, complementary colors, close/far)?
- Are the points of interest clearly defined?
- Are the strong lines leading the viewer's eye to the focal points?
- Is there a sense of organized movement throughout the painting? Have you guided the viewer's eye towards interesting areas?

FIGURE 6.18 Digital painting done in Photoshop for *Assassin's Creed Valhalla* (*Assassin's Creed* TM & © Ubisoft Entertainment. All Rights Reserved).

- Have you created an entrance point in the painting?
- Is there a clear distinction between foreground, midground, and background?
- Have you avoided drawing too much attention to the edges and corners of the picture plane?
- Are the color temperatures appropriate? Can you introduce more interesting variations? Where should it be cooler or warmer? Does the color palette have a dominant warm or cool tone?

FIGURE 6.19 Digital painting done in Photoshop for *Assassin's Creed Unity* (*Assassin's Creed* TM & © Ubisoft Entertainment. All Rights Reserved).

- How about the saturation and hues of colors? Does it match the desired mood or feeling?
- Have you used details effectively? Do you need all those details everywhere, or can you simplify some areas while enhancing others?
- Can you refine the edges further? Can you vary between hard, firm, soft, and lost edges?
- Are the shapes well defined? Can you make them cleaner and more accurate?
- Are there any 'pinches' in the direction of your lines? Can you improve the design of some objects?
- Should you consider cropping the painting to see how it affects it?

Don't hesitate to refer to this checklist when feeling stuck; it proves to be very useful.

FIGURE 6.20 Digital painting done in Photoshop for *Assassin's Creed III* (*Assassin's Creed* TM & © Ubisoft Entertainment. All Rights Reserved).

FIGURE 7.1 Digital sketch done in Photoshop for *For Honor* (© Ubisoft Entertainment. All Rights Reserved).

CHAPTER 7

Skills to Work On

DOI: 10.1201/9781003536703-8

THE IMPORTANCE OF ROUTINE TO AVOID PROCRASTINATION

When painting becomes your profession, there are those days when you don't feel inspired, when it's hard to get started, or when you feel like you won't achieve anything good.

This happens regularly, and you can call it lacking inspiration. In fact, inspiration comes when you're ready to welcome it. You might operate a bit like a diesel engine and sometimes struggle to reach your cruising speed. In such cases, start by painting easier things, correcting errors from the previous day you notice in your painting or adding a detail here and there. Then, you'll notice that you get into a flow and inspiration comes as you work, when you let go a little. Try to identify the moments in your day when you're at your best and organize your week accordingly. Try to have a sort of work routine, always starting at the same time and rarely making exceptions. Build a consistent work habit. It is not enough to overcome procrastination once. You must do it daily for years. This is how you build anything successful.

FIGURE 7.2 Digital painting done in Photoshop for *Assassin's Creed Origins* (*Assassin's Creed* TM & © Ubisoft Entertainment. All Rights Reserved).

ANATOMY

When designing an environment, it's always beneficial to introduce a character, as mentioned earlier. This not only enriches the storytelling but, more importantly, provides a clear sense of scale—an essential element in environment design.

Even if your main interest lies in environment design, developing your anatomy knowledge is highly valuable. The benefits are numerous: First, it pushes you out of your comfort zone, which is always a catalyst for growth. Second, studying anatomy improves your overall drawing skills—mastering the human figure often sharpens your ability to draw almost anything. And finally, it enhances your painting process, allowing you to sketch characters more confidently within your scenes—a significant advantage. It is recommended to at least know the basics of human anatomy. This way, you can spot anomalies, proportion issues, and be able to paint your characters in interesting poses. At the very least, avoid ruining a beautiful environment painting by adding a character that looks awkward or has a boring pose.

FIGURE 7.3 An example of studies done to improve drawing and anatomy: studying hands in John Singer Sargent's paintings.

To work on your anatomy skills, the best option, of course, would be to enroll in life drawing sessions with live models. Interpreting volumes into 2D shapes is more formative than drawing from photos.

If you plan to focus on your drawing in your spare time without really planning, you can draw from videos of live models that you can easily find online. Another way is to buy specialized books on anatomy and character design and copy all the drawings in them, while trying to understand the mechanics of the human (or animal) body. All these techniques will help you progress.

If, on the other hand, your goal is to become a character designer, you can never know too much about anatomy. Learning absolutely everything possible about the mechanics of the human and animal body should be, in this case, your number one priority. On the other hand, most of the information on digital painting techniques that you find in this book is, of course, still valid, whether you are painting an environment or a character.

PERSPECTIVE

If you want to specialize in environment concept art, you need to have at least a good understanding of the basic rules of perspective. Perspective is a tool for creating the illusion of depth in your digital painting. As we have already seen, other tools include overlapping, atmospheric perspective, and the fact that objects close to the viewer appear larger than the same objects in the distance.

Of course, being able to create a 3D layout will help in situations where calculating perspective is laborious, such as when trying to draw complex architecture with a short camera lens (which distorts shapes and perspective). However, in some situations, you might need to do paint overs (painting over a game screenshot), sketches, or add elements to a painting, and in these cases, you must know what perspective to use.

FIGURE 7.4A An example of work that may be requested during a video game production: a screenshot of a location that needs to be redesigned or dressed up. You then must paint over it.

Designing the horizon line and vanishing points are the basic elements to know regarding perspective. The first thing to do is to try to identify where the horizon line is. For this, try to imagine that the image you are creating was taken by someone with a camera, and ask yourself: What height is the camera? If the camera is high relative to the scene, then the horizon line is high. If, on the contrary, the camera seems low relative to the scene (a low-angle view), then the horizon line will be low. Easy!

FIGURE 7.4B After observation, you can see that the horizon line should be approximately at this location. If you imagine someone taking this photo, you can clearly see that he is below the platform level but above the water level, as the tops of the first steps of the staircase are visible.

Second, ask yourself which elements have parallel lines. The lines for painting these elements will all converge at the same point on the horizon line, if they are also parallel to the ground. This is called a *vanishing point.* You will most often need to designate multiple vanishing points, as, most of the time, the lines of the elements you are painting are not all parallel.

FIGURE 7.4C All parallel lines converge toward the same vanishing point. If they are also parallel to the ground, this vanishing point will be located on the horizon line. Note that the vanishing point can be outside the frame.

For more intense viewing angles, such as strong low or high angles, it will also be necessary to designate what is called a third vanishing point to guide the lines of parallel objects pointing up or down.

FIGURE 7.4D Here, you can see that the vertical lines are not parallel to the edges of the image; instead, they converge toward a point located above the 'imaginary cameraman'. This is another vanishing point. The shorter the lens, the closer to the frame this point will be. If you want a long focal length effect, you should only use straight lines parallel to the edges of the image. This will 'flatten' the perspective effect. In summary: A short focal length creates significant distortion (but covers more space), and a long focal length flattens perspective and depth (but requires a good distance, as it captures a narrower field of view). Keep these concepts in mind when drawing your vanishing lines.

FIGURE 7.4E Here is the result. With the help of the perspective lines, it was easier to paint new elements, especially architectural ones (Digital painting done in Photoshop for *Assassin's Creed Origins, Assassin's Creed* TM & © Ubisoft Entertainment. All Rights Reserved).

A little trick to keep in mind when you paint a scene from an eye-level position: Ensure that the heads of all the characters in the scene are approximately aligned at the same height. It is the rest of the body that appears at different heights.

FIGURE 7.5 Notice how the characters' heads are approximately at the same height relative to one another and follow a line—the horizon line—since you can imagine that your imaginary photographer has a viewpoint at human eye level. Taller characters will be above this line, while shorter ones will be below it. The distance between the head and the feet indicates how far those characters are (Digital painting done in Photoshop for *Assassin's Creed Unity, Assassin's Creed* TM & © Ubisoft Entertainment. All Rights Reserved).

To delve deeper, refer to books specialized in the subject. Just like human anatomy, this subject is very vast and would deserve a book of its own.

FIGURE 7.6 For this digital painting, no 3D models were used—a notable choice, especially for a scene featuring complex architecture where a 3D base is often recommended as a drawing reference. Instead, the composition was built entirely using vanishing point guides to establish perspective (Digital painting done for *Assassin's Creed Valhalla*, *Assassin's Creed* TM & © Ubisoft Entertainment. All Rights Reserved).

DRAW FROM AN IMAGE OR PHOTO

Drawing from an image or a photo is a good exercise that will help you progress in several areas. First, it will improve your ability to accurately replicate a shape through drawing. The more you practice, the more accurate and better you will become at it. Additionally, it will enhance your skills in design (if you copy objects or vehicles) or anatomy (if you copy characters, animals, or creatures). It will also help you become familiar with specific styles (manga, cartoons, comics, realism, etc.). Try to vary the styles of illustrations you copy. For example, if you only copy manga illustrations, you will develop a style very specific to that genre but may struggle with more realistic proportions. Another advantage of drawing from images or photos is that it will enrich the image bank in your mind, making it more robust when you need it—such as when drawing from your imagination.

DO STUDIES OF IMAGES

This practice is very important and highly recommended, especially when you are beginning your journey as a digital painter. Choose a painting, a concept art piece, or an image from a film and try to copy it as accurately as you can. Aim to match the values, colors, and, of course, the shapes. This exercise is incredibly instructive and very encouraging because you will see satisfying results quite quickly. If your drawing skills are still developing, don't hesitate to draw a grid on both your reference image and your canvas; this will help you copy the shapes more accurately. After some time, you won't need the grid anymore. This habit of studying masterpieces will help you improve in all areas.

FIGURE 7.7 Would you like to copy this painting? (Digital painting done in Photoshop for *Assassin's Creed Unity* (*Assassin's Creed* TM & © Ubisoft Entertainment. All Rights Reserved)).

PAINT FROM LIFE

It is one of the best ways to progress, whether in drawing or painting. It seems more instructive and challenging than drawing from a photo because you have an additional step to perform in your head: You need to interpret a 3D form, a volume, into a 2D shape. You also need to interpret the values you see and try to simplify them as much as possible. It's difficult exercise, but it will help you improve immensely.

If you want to increase the difficulty even further, try plein air painting. This is like an extreme sport. Not only do you have to make the interpretations described above, interpret the colors you see and choose a palette, but you also have to deal with changing light (Claude Monet said that light remains relatively stable for about twenty minutes, no more), possible changes in lighting with passing clouds, wind, insects, and curious onlookers, not to mention the difficulty of setting up and transporting your painted canvas. In short, it's not as relaxing as one might imagine, but it is a worthwhile experience just for the opportunity to be focused on and admire nature for a good while. And of course, this will feed your personal visual library, enabling you to paint from your imagination in a more interesting and faithful manner to reality.

FIGURE 7.8 An example of a still life painting created outdoors.

Conclusion

FIGURE 8.1 Digital painting done for *Assassin's Creed Origins* (*Assassin's Creed* TM & © Ubisoft Entertainment. All Rights Reserved).

SKILLS AT DOING VERSUS SKILLS AT SEEING

Throughout your life as an artist, you're bound to experience moments of discouragement. It's inevitable. You'll notice flaws in your digital paintings and feel like you'll never be good enough. This has probably happened to you already. However, if you compare your current work with what you were doing ten years ago, there's a good chance you'll see improvement (assuming you continued to paint and/or draw during that time, of course). On the other hand, there will be moments when you feel like you've finally grasped the secrets of painting and believe you're at the top of your game (though these moments are quite rare, to be honest). The frustrating part is that you can frequently swing between these states, but how is that possible?

DOI: 10.1201/9781003536703-9

FIGURE 8.2 Digital painting done for *For Honor* (© Ubisoft Entertainment. All Rights Reserved).

You need to understand one thing. Over the years of practice, you acquire the ability to create art and the ability to see errors in your work (and in others' work). When your ability to see these errors is more advanced than your ability to create art, you'll feel down and think you're not good enough.

Conversely, if your ability to create art is at a higher level than your ability to spot errors, you'll feel like you're finally a good artist. Keep this in mind when you don't understand why your work isn't being recognized or when you think you'll never make it. You're simply in one of these phases in your learning path.

The most important thing to understand is that, regardless of what you think, you are progressing if you practice. It's not in a regular pattern; there are plateaus and peaks, but you are making progress over the years, if you continue to draw and paint.

Sometimes, you'll feel like you're not progressing, that you're stagnant, or even regressing, especially when comparing your current work to previous pieces.

FIGURE 8.3 Digital painting done for *For Honor* (© Ubisoft Entertainment. All Rights Reserved).

If this happens, it's likely because you've recently learned or understood new concepts, and your brain needs time to process this new information, which it tends to focus on for a while. The good news is that these plateaus are often followed by significant progress.

However, be aware that the further you advance in your career, the longer these plateaus can last. This is why it's important not to fall into a routine with your techniques and to constantly try new things, even though it's difficult when working on a production where efficiency is key. That's not really the time to experiment. Hence, the importance of practicing in your personal time, to learn new concepts and techniques that you can later incorporate into your work routine.

FIGURE 8.4 Digital painting done for *Assassin's Creed Syndicate* (*Assassin's Creed* TM & © Ubisoft Entertainment. All Rights Reserved).

DON'T STOP!

It's a marathon, not a sprint. There are highs and lows, accelerations, moments when you move forward without feeling like you're trying, and others when it feels like you're slowing down even though you're going full speed. The important thing, even though moments of discouragement are inevitable, is not to stop. A person who stops drawing or painting, will instantly stop progressing. You can see evidence of this if you observe grown-ups who haven't drawn since they were children. Well, you'll notice that they draw like children! It's not because they're not talented; it's just that they've maintained the level they had the day they stopped drawing. But don't blame yourself if you feel inadequate or discouraged; it still happens to experienced artists. You just need to have a routine, change tasks. For example, stop drawing live models and start drawing photos and pictures you find in encyclopedias. It's different, it changes, you still learn to copy shapes, and at the same time, you learn how certain objects are designed. When you no longer find pleasure in this, you'll find something else but always for the same purpose: to improve your drawing skills and feed your personal image bank that you store somewhere in your mind and that will allow you to create, later, an image from your imagination.

FIGURE 8.5 Digital painting done in Photoshop for *Assassin's Creed Valhalla* (*Assassin's Creed* TM & © Ubisoft Entertainment. All Rights Reserved)

PASSION VERSUS PATIENCE

If you've been that far in this book, it's probably because you're passionate about visual art and you either are or aspire to become an artist. This passion is very important; it will help you overcome periods of discouragement that seem inevitable. You wish you could be as good as your favorite artists, but you probably never will be, or if you do reach that level, those artists will be replaced by others in your mind. There will always be someone better than you, and this quest to become as good as a particular artist should remain healthy and motivate you to double your efforts. But don't think you'll reach a good level in a day or even in a year. It will take years (decades?) before you reach a level you find acceptable.

FIGURE 8.6 Digital painting done in Photoshop for *For Honor* (© Ubisoft Entertainment. All Rights Reserved).

Therefore, don't see this goal as the moment when you will finally fulfill yourself as an artist. Instead, enjoy the journey that will take you there. It's an exciting path that will take you through different phases in your style, which you will see evolve despite yourself. Moments of discouragement are inevitable, as are failures. But they are there to help you grow, and sometimes the results take a long time to come, but they will inevitably come. And it's the passion you feel that will help you overcome these obstacles. Ask yourself why you want to pursue this profession. If it's to become famous, or for money, it's not a good idea. If it's to feel the joy you felt as a child when you used to imagine worlds coming to life through your pencils or brushes, then you seem equipped to overcome these obstacles and thrive as an artist because you are where you are meant to be. The road is long and full of hurdles, but the reward of being able to do a job you love is immense.

FIGURE 8.7 Digital painting done for *Assassin's Creed Unity* (*Assassin's Creed* TM & © Ubisoft Entertainment. All Rights Reserved).

IMPORTANCE OF YOUR PORTFOLIO

Forget about diplomas (except sometimes for obtaining work visas if you plan to work abroad). To find a job or a collaboration on a project, you need a portfolio that shows your best work. An Art Director looking for an artist will browse through online portfolios and contact artists who seem to have a style that matches the project they're working on. Therefore, your portfolio should always be up to date with your best work; it's your showcase. Focus on quality rather than quantity. Show the things you enjoy working on the most. For example, if you want to become a character designer, showcase that in your portfolio. Show, for instance, 90% of character drawings/paintings and 10% of other things (such as environments or props). Don't include things you don't enjoy doing or aren't very comfortable with because someone might call you to do just that for the next two years. Show some sketches, iterations and processes as well. Art Directors love that.

FIGURE 8.8 Digital painting done in Photoshop for *For Honor* (© Ubisoft Entertainment. All Rights Reserved).

RESOURCES

If you dream of becoming an artist, it's likely because certain artists have inspired you so deeply that you feel compelled to follow in their footsteps. Their mastery, their ability to simplify complex values, and the power of their epic compositions—each element lights a spark in you. You want to reach that level of skill, and more importantly, to feel the same joy they seemed to experience while creating their masterpieces.

To help you on that path, here are some essential resources, additionally to this book, that can expand your understanding of painting and drawing, among other valuable artistic skills:

Alla Prima II: Everything I Know about Painting—And More by Richard Schmid

All the videos of demos done by Richard Schmid (richardschmid.com).

Composition of Outdoor Painting by Edgar Payne

Framed Ink: Drawing and Composition for Visual Storytellers by Marcos Mateu-Mestre

Dream Worlds: Production Design for Animation: Production Design in Animation by Hans Bacher

All Andrew Loomis's books

All the tutorial videos of demos done by Quang Ho (mfa.studio/videos)

ANATOMY DRAWING CLASS by Rockhe Kim

Constructive Anatomy by George B. Bridgman

Devin Korwin's learning material (underpaintacademy.com)

The following online schools: Proko, New Masters Academy, Schoolism, Made for Artists (mfa), etc.

Good luck and have fun!

FIGURE 8.9 Digital painting done for *Assassin's Creed Unity* (*Assassin's Creed* TM & © Ubisoft Entertainment. All Rights Reserved).

Acknowledgements

"Special thanks to my parents, my wife, and my children for their constant support. Thanks also to Florence Baccard, Élyse Canuel, and Sébastien Signoret at Ubisoft Montreal, as well as Sean Connelly, Migien Mocke, Alyss Barraza, Danielle Zarfati, and Balaji Karuppanan for helping make this book a reality."

Index